Online Collaborative Learning:

Challenges and Opportunities
for NGOs in Developing Countries

Online Collaborative Learning

Challenges and Opportunities
for NGOs in Developing Countries

KENDAY SAMUEL KAMARA

Dignity Press
World Dignity University Press

Published by Dignity Press 2013
16 Northview Court
Lake Oswego, OR 97035, USA
www.dignitypress.org

Book website: www.dignitypress.org/ocl
Pre-media: Uli Spalthoff

Printed on paper from environmentally managed forestry:
www.lightningsource.com/chainofcustody

ISBN 978-1-937570-21-7
Also available as EPUB: ISBN 978-1-937570-22-4
and Kindle eBook: ISBN 978-1-937570-23-1

Contents

Preface

The unlimited possibilities and the political in technological faith

After seven years of research—as a self-fulfilling enlightenment—this book remains my favorite work. Despite its overreaching ambition and technological grand revolution, this text lays bare the fundamental expectations of my faith in technology: to plumb the depths of technology in order to disclose the fascinating truths of our modern human achievements. My work on online collaborative learning (OCL) rests upon two assumptions of modern times—that OCL technology offers unlimited possibilities and that their strengths and limits have something distinctive to say about what it means to run a modern, technologically empowered institution. Yet this work is not simply interpretive, analytical or poetic in aim—it also seeks to be political in its attempt to enrich and enable the power of technology in making institutions stronger.

Non-governmental organizations (NGOs) have become crucial to the struggle for greater economic and social justice in the world, especially in developing countries. What these organizations have in common is the need to expand their capabilities through training and education which creates new knowledge. Online Collaborative Learning (OCL) has proven itself to be effective in economically advanced countries and can be just as effective in developing countries as access to the necessary technological infrastructure develops—if people like you and others help. The book thus provides theoretical frameworks, research methodologies, and potential strategies for promoting and developing the use of OCL by NGOs working in developing countries.

Although my explicit intention in this book was to put forward a prophetic interpretation of the technological magic, informed by innovative software programming and pragmatic thought, my underlying motivation was to understand the complexities and ambiguities of modernity through the lens of an educated mind within the OCL environments of the University of Phoenix and Walden University. In other words, I tried to conceive of OCL technology in the light of its ability to have condensed planet Earth into a cozy community of seven billion citizens, and it is shrinking by the nanosecond; and a learning experience at best. Needless to say, OCL technology is more than simply modern or an epitome of western civilization. Today, mankind's neighborhoods have transcended physical boundaries, as people console each other in chat rooms, blather in blogospheres, and are probably more likely to be in constant contact with a friend who lives across the country than one across the street. OCL technology has become the primary agent through which we interpret western modernity and technologically advanced humanity—building on the pioneering work of especially the great Silicon Valley IT wizards. My effort to articulate an OCL philosophy was predicated on the notion that OCL—mediated through Internet technology and interactive realities—had significant insight for the human as a social being and his quest for wisdom. People are LinkedIn, YouTubed, Twittered, Facebooked, BlackBerry-ed and Googled at all hours of the day and night. From spanning the globe to find soul mates (mailorderhusband.net), to hiring a personal assistant in India for as little as seven dollars an hour (taskeveryday.com), the power to improve human lives and livelihoods, is but a keystroke away. The world today is swimming in a cyber-fishbowl.

Thus, this book is primarily a sociological interpretation of OCL capabilities—shot through with in-depth research work and hands-on ends—that tries to promote OCL technology in order to inspire productive action on NGOs for a better world. The unlimited possibilities of OCL are not to predict technological outcomes but rather to identify concrete possibilities. The unlimited OCL capabilities essential to NGO productivity are not to disregard the traditional roles of NGOs but rather to generate enough faith, hope and innovation to sustain the human possibility for more productivity. For me, to be a community of practice facilitator is not to opt for some basic knowledge or amateurish obligation but rather to confront the deeper social action and the human innovative spirit of NGOs with the strong armor of research and development which can be very useful in making NGOs in developing countries more vibrant and productive. NGOs quest for OCL knowledge and flexibility provide some crucial insight and inspiration regarding these unfathomable possibilities of OCL technology

Digital Culture and Technologies

Online collaborative learning (OCL) is a significant part of information and communication technology (ICT). Users can examine how digital culture and digital technologies have rapidly become unavoidable and essential forms of social experience and communication in the globalized society. The range of possibilities OCL and ICTs have offered in terms of empowering NGOs in developing countries made even more critical by the rapid growth of the Internet and the needs of a mobile society is considered in this work. The popularity of OCL, the mobility of today's NGOs globally, and the increasing access to high speed Internet communication has made resolving the problems with OCL critical to today's knowledge building community. A further examination of how computer-based technologies have become more and more dynamic and much less controlled by political systems; recognizing, however, that the orderly and efficient development of telecommunications infrastructures in developing countries is necessary to keep pace with development with other sectors of economies.

Accountability mechanisms

With the widespread use and expansion of new public management systems, developed western countries have seen acceptable improvements in their societies due to the incorporation of accountability mechanisms using OCL tools in their systems. Modern public administration is not just about efficiency; it also involves ideas of democratic participation, accountability and empowerment. There is, therefore, a constant tension between two main themes: making government efficient and keeping government accountable. The influential model of new public management promises to integrate these themes, linking efficiency and accountability together. The 'new public management revolution' has sparked unprecedented interest in attempts to reshape and improve governance, defined as the array of ways in which the relationships between the state, society and the market is ordered. With OCL's universal appeal, NGOs in developing countries can now develop meaningful relationships with their international partners by also incorporating similar accountability mechanisms with OCL tools in their systems. Trust among development partners facilitates long-term social change. Examples of mechanisms and technologies with various capabilities are considered.

Kenday Samuel Kamara, Ph.D.

Denver, Colorado
February 2013

Acknowledgements

This book on *OCL: Challenges and Opportunities for NGOs in Developing Countries* is the result of shared experiences, relationships and thoughts with many people over a long time. I am deeply indebted to all those who nurtured this project in ways large and small from the moment of inception to the moment of completing the book. It won't be possible to acknowledge all of those persons who had made contributions to the research work of this book. Researching a book requires assistance from so many individuals and sources. I wish to thank, however, a few who were especially helpful.

This book was supported by various material and scholarly contributions made by my colleagues at the Center for Development & Business Research (CODBRA). The book draws upon a myriad of user studies and client projects conducted by members of the Center for Development & Business Research, and my insights have been honed by many discussions with this group of supremely talented professionals. I would have no data if it weren't for my faithful colleagues at the Center in Denver who gave themselves unselfishly in the form of close textual scrutiny and intellectual encouragement. And special thanks to Daru Archrekar, CPA, and Paula Kerstein, MBA, for help with the manuscript and providing encouragement that allowed me to complete this book.

For both sections of the book, I am especially indebted to Dr. Marc Bélanger, Coordinator of Akcio-International[1] and associate member of the World Congress of NGOs who encouraged me to collaborate

---

1   Akcio is an NGO of educators and technology designers dedicated to the development of online collaborative learning pedagogies and technologies for developing countries. It is based in South Africa, Brazil, Italy and Canada. Akcio is the Esperanto word for "sharing". Retrieved from: http:// www.akcio-int.org

with a group of professors: Dr. Indrajit Bhattacharya, Professor and Academic In-charge, International Institute of Health Management Research, India; Dr. Linda Harasim, Professor, Simon Fraser University, Canada; Dr. Bolanle Olaniran, Interim Chair and Professor, Department of Communication Studies, Texas Tech University, U.S.A.; Mr. Tim Roberts, Professor, Central Queensland University, Australia; Dr. Hari Srinivas, Coordinator, Global Development Research Centre; and Dr. Lucio Teles, Professor Universidade de Brasilia, Brazil; to contribute to a book to be published by IGI Global on the topic of *"Online Collaborative Learning for Non-governmental Organizations in Developing Countries: Issues and Challenges."* The ultimate organization of this work is therefore a result of the collaboration inspired by Dr. Bélanger; and the work itself is drawn from seven years of applied research on the use of OCL technologies. Further, even though IGI Global did not get to publish the intended book, the body of work contained in this volume was instead peer-reviewed by this group of distinguished professors.

Never before in history has innovation offered promise of so much to so many in so short a time.

Bill Gates

This is perhaps the most beautiful time in human history; it is really pregnant with all kinds of creative possibilities made possible by science and technology which now constitute the slave of man—if man is not enslaved by it.

Jonas Salk

Part I:

Digital Culture and Technologies as Essential Forms of Online Collaborative Learning for NGOs in Developing Countries

Introduction

Online collaborative learning (OCL) emerged as a significant part of information and communication technology (ICT) during the latter part of the twentieth century (Tomei, 2009). OCL is as central and dominant in the advancement of ICTs today as at the field's conception because of the involvement of non-state or non-governmental actors in policy-making in a consultative way or through the development of new participatory approaches. Essentially, in the last decade various forms of electronic communication platforms have proliferated. These platforms have facilitated electronic communication globally. The global adoption of dedicated bulletin boards or discussion forums, incorporated within web-based products such as WebCT[2], FirstClass[3] and BlackBoard[4] have created many possibilities. These dedicated bulletin boards provide great opportunities for the development of what can be referred to as knowledge-building communities (Bereiter & Scardamalia, 2003)—with a real sense of community amongst people and provide opportunities to effectively engage in cooperative discussions. OCL allows users to examine how digital culture and digital technologies have rapidly become unavoidable and essential forms of social experience and communication in the globalized society. It hinges on the notion that if researchers want to attempt to analyze and

---

2   WebCT (Course Tools) or Blackboard Learning System, now owned by Blackboard, is an online proprietary virtual learning environment system that is sold to colleges and other institutions and used in many campuses for e-learning. Retrieved from http://en.wikipedia.org/wiki/WebCT

3   Open Text FirstClass® is a fully integrated suite of applications designed to enhance communication, collaboration, and knowledge sharing. First-Class includes components such as email and instant messaging, calendaring, contacts, personal web publishing, online workspaces, file storage, and more - all fully customizable and accessible from a single desktop . Retrieved from http://www.firstclass.com/

4   BlackBoard works with more than 5,000 institutions and millions of users to focus on a single mission: to increase the impact of education by transforming the experience of education. Retrieved from http://www. blackboard.com/

understand the technology-saturated society with its new media, then they must also employ research methods and forms of analysis that can accommodate and exploit digital culture and digital technologies. Competency in the use of computer based communication technology has also become critical and represents a heightening of the information technology agenda.

Online collaborative learning offers a range of possibilities for NGOs in developing countries. The rapid growth of the Internet and the needs of a mobile society have made OCL critical for the empowerment of NGOs. The growing importance of OCL is a quite likely trajectory that will continue during the next decade. OCL presents many advantages. These include the convenience of asynchronous participation, a permanent record of active learning, and analysis tools (Bhattacharaya, 1999). Like any new technology, it takes research and experimentation over a period of time to implement various OCL innovations and optimize them. Of course, more research, experimentation and better tools are needed to accommodate the maximum potential processes of what OCL have to offer.

Considerable studies have been done on methods of online collaborative learning and similar systems. Among the earliest were the electronic information exchange system (EIES) experiments conducted in the National Science Foundation (NSF) in the late 1970's by Hiltz and Turoff (1978). These experiments by Hiltz and Turoff (1977) studied methods of making group decisions and collaborating on projects and documents. Since then, a proliferation of OCL platforms is seen. The popularity of OCL, the mobility of today's NGOs globally, and the increasing access to high speed Internet communication have made resolving the problems with OCL critical to today's knowledge building community. Several existing models of media communication platforms attest to the impact that such networks can have on global governance. OCL is one of several mechanisms been set up that allow organizations to assemble and distribute multiple comments and then produce an integrated and consensus-based reply (Dillenbourg & Schneider, 1995).

Today, the Internet revolution has brought ever-changing business websites, inexpensive e-zines, blogging and social networking sites, such as MySpace and Facebook—all of which are rapidly changing the way the world communicates. The proliferation of information technologies thus suggests a phenomenal progression in people-to-people communication and a decentralization of communication away from old vertical patterns of broadcasting systems. With computer-based technologies, communication is becoming more and more dynamic and much less controlled by political systems. The capacity for North-South and South-South communication is even more transforming as people in different developing regions forge new relationships and alliances (Smillie & Hailey, 2001). Populations with access to these new communications and information technologies are becoming more and more empowered. Political systems can no longer be the all-powerful watchdogs that regulate the information people receive, nor monitor or stifle how people communicate with each other. The impact these new knowledge networks have on economic development, on political organizations, and socio-cultural value systems of societies is unparalleled. There exists an effective relationship between technology and society. Communication networks make societies dynamic. With ICT networks people cooperate, they produce and exchange commodities, they share ideas and information. ICTs have a catalytic effect on the development of other sectors of economies such as agriculture, health, tourism and education and their necessity for the commercial, industrial, socio-economic and political development of countries; as such the orderly and efficient development of telecommunications infrastructures in developing countries is necessary to keep pace with development with other sectors of economies (Buck, Wollenberg & Edmunds, 2001).

However, ICTs call for sound investment decisions, technological and management innovations, operational and financial efficiency. UNESCO's New Information and Communications Order in 1976 (Preston & Herman, 1989) validated many developing countries' interest in receiving foreign aid to develop their information and communication infrastructures. Aid programs were established in the fields of mass media and telecommunications development. Higher priority was granted to investment in telecommunications, new methods of financing such projects in developing countries were considered, and the International

Telecommunication Union (ITU) was given an effective role in ICT development. In Africa, the Lagos Plan of Action[5] for the Economic Development of Africa which incorporated in its program of action, the Transport and Communications Decade for Africa[6], dealt with various aspects of telecommunications development plans. In sum, information and communication technology has shown the potential to condition power, knowledge and creativity. Though unevenly distributed within countries and between countries, information and communication technology still passes as an essential tool for economic development and material well-being.

---

5   The Organization of African Unity Lagos Plan of Action for the Economic Development of Africa, 1980-2000. Republished by the United Nations Economic Commission for Africa.
Retrieved http://www.uneca.org/itca/ariportal/docs/lagos_plan.pdf
6   The program of the second United Nations Transport and Communications Decade in Africa (UNTACDA II) has been under implementation since 1991. The long-term aims of the second Decade are to establish an efficient integrated transport and communications system as a basis for the physical integration of Africa, so as to facilitate traffic movement, foster trade and enable the achievement of self- sustained economic development as envisaged in the Abuja Treaty establishing the African Economic Community.
Retrieved http://www.uneca.org/cfm/21/ecamin_t.htm

The medium, or process, of our time—electric technology is reshaping and restructuring patterns of social interdependence and every aspect of our personal life. It is forcing us to reconsider and re-evaluate practically every thought, every action,"

Marshall McLuhan

The key is the Internet. The United States is by far the most advanced country in this new digital culture, so we have to be there. The Internet is the heart of this new civilization, and telecommunications are the nervous system, or circulatory system.

Carlos Slim Helu

Chapter 1: What is Online Collaborative Learning?

Online Collaborative Learning (OCL) is a space or online environment, usually enabled by software on a computer network, designed to facilitate the transfer and sharing of knowledge among participating users of the network (Harasim, *et. al.*, 1995). It is an asynchronous learning network (ALN) that has grown both in use, popularity and power (Benbunan & Hiltz, 1999). Dringus and Terrell (1998) have defined OCL as "...a distinct, pedagogically meaningful and comprehensive online learning environment by which learners and faculty can participate in the learning and instructional process at any time and any place." OCL, however, is not just a tool in the traditional sense of pedagogy. OCL is a knowledge-sharing environment that is reciprocal among participants exerting positive influences on themselves (Sherry & Wilson, 1997). OCL is collaborative learning which allows for scaffolding of thinking and knowledge shared and recognizes immediacy of feedback (Siegel & Kirkley, 1997). It is a knowledge-management environment that promotes behaviors that illustrate categorical social collaboration in creating and sharing information, exchanging resources and feedback, contemplating on process and progress, and supporting measurable mutual goals (Srikantaiah & Koenig, 2008).

Information and Communication Technologies (ICTs) are technologies that support OCL systems and the storage and transmission of information. ICTs are often identified as "leapfrogging" technologies, an amalgam of rapidly advancing technologies which give individuals new capabilities for accessing information as well as for inter-personal communication (Quibria, 2002). ICTs applications and networks include electronic networks—embodying complex hardware and software—linked by a vast array of technical protocols (Verdejo, 1996). ICTs are embedded in networks and services that affect the local and global accumulation and flow of public and private information and knowledge. They are supported by network technologies and spatial information systems such as e-mail, listserves, electronic bulletins, web sites, video conferencing, computer networks, mobile cell phones, and CD-ROM technology. ICTs are transforming ways in which governments, the private sector and individuals work. ICTs influence on humanity has been revolutionary. ICTs are a general purpose technology, and their impact in economies is pervasive in the ICT-capital goods producing sector and the increasing accumulation and application of ICT-goods and services in the user sectors (Keen, Brown & Dyball, 2005). ICTs permit information and knowledge to expand in quantity and accessibility through faster generation, manipulation and transmission of information. ICTs thus offer new opportunities for social and economic transformation.

The 1998/99 World Bank World Development Report[7], subtitled *Knowledge and Information for Development*, recognized the transformation potential of ICTs. The report saw the explosion of digital resources reflecting the rapid embracing of new knowledge tools, the accelerating technological progress, and the ever-increasing competition as more important than ever. ICTs are seen to offer developing countries unprecedented opportunities to enhance educational systems, improve policy formation and execution, and widen the range of opportunities for business and the poor.

According to the United Nations Development Program (UNDP), "ICTs, can involve more people, hitherto unreached or under-serviced. ICTs allow access to information sources worldwide; promote networking transcending borders, languages and cultures, foster empowerment of communities, women, youth and socially disadvantaged groups"(Smillie, 1999).

The revolutionary advancement of ICTs is even believed to have contributed in many ways to the development of a new *'diplomacy of human rights'* to the extent that the International Telecommunications Union

---

7   The 1998-99 World Development Report states that knowledge, not capital, is the key to sustained economic growth and improvements in human well-being. It distinguishes between two sorts of knowledge: knowledge about technology, called technical knowledge or simply know-how, and knowledge about attributes, that is, knowledge about products, processes, or institutions. The report focuses on the relationship between the unequal distribution in know-how (knowledge gaps) across and within countries and the difficulties posed by having incomplete knowledge of attributes (information problems).

(ITU) has recognized the global significance of the 'right to communicate' as a part of the principles embodied in the Universal Declaration of Human Rights. The vast potential of ICT and OCL in an information society that has today become so global offer developing countries unprecedented opportunities to enhance educational systems, improve policy formation and execution, and widen the range of opportunities for business and the poor. Individuals, NGOs, national governments, and supranational institutions have all been empowered insofar as they have the means to effectively communicate their stories, agendas, laws and agreements, respectively and with maximum impact (see Table below for international sector analysis vis-à-vis ICT applications).

ICTs thus offer opportunity for effective working modalities across NGOs and government agencies and are effective as a force for human rights, providing a global platform for opposition movements challenging autocratic regimes and military dictatorships. The evolving relationships of civil society entities with one other—as enhanced and strengthened by ICTs—are significant to any analysis of governance.

International Entities and [Some] ICT Applications

Sectors	ICT Applications
Individuals	Empowered through the use of [wire line] and wireless communication (voice and SMS/data, email, the Internet (with access to reporting procedures like the Options Protocol under CCPI), as well as [internet] radio/television [services].
Activist NGOs	Empowered through the use of Internet, email, and wireless communications to contact media, other NGOs, national governments, and supranational governing bodies from all locations; ICTs have facilitated transnational networking as well as fundraising.
National Governments	Practice traditional forms of public diplomacy (including traditional broadcast (unidirectional media like TV and radio), and utilize networked communications for enhancing transparency and access to laws and national policies, surveillance, administration, and many more.
Supranational governing bodies	Use communications to optimize engagement of member states in international organizations, and for consultation with major non-governmental organizations, as well for heightening accessibility of all to international documentation of treaties, accords, agreements and international dispute settlement.

Note: From "ICTs in Support of Human Rights, Democracy and Good Governance" by A. N. Selian, 2002, retrieved from http://www.itu.int/osg/spu/wsis-themes/humanrights/ICTs%20and%20HR.pdf. Copyright 2002 by International Communications Union[8].

---

8   The International Telecommunication Union (ITU) is the leading United Nations agency for information and communication technology issues, and

OCL Research and Development

OCL technologies usage by non-governmental organizations is an emergent field of research. Several studies have demonstrated that many NGOs and broader civil society in developing regions of the world are still in early stage of IT adoption on their organizational settings (Kelly, 2005). Evidently, many studies have considered important perspectives on key trends and developments in ICT-knowledge networks and how collaboration, mentoring and community can be used to energize e-knowledge management.

The field of organizational learning itself has been a central discourse within the NGO literature, and there is a conventional perspective that has become apparent that preceding perspectives on NGOs as learning organizations, introduced by early scholars of NGO development studies such as Korten (1990), may not be applicable as a rule across the broad spectrum of the development NGO field. Indeed, another NGO scholar, Fowler (1997), alludes to the argument about, "an almost universal weakness of NGOs is found within their often-limited capacity to learn, adapt and continuously improve the quality of what they do, [which Fowler explains] is a serious concern" (p.64). The problem is that NGOs generally seem to lack effective information systems that can provide access to data about what they are doing and thereby enable them to access what they are not achieving. Via this evaluative exercise, lessons can be distilled effectively into future planning and practice. If anything could be done, there has to be some volume of investment made by NGOs in OCL technologies, which allows the collection of

---

the global focal point for governments and the private sector in developing networks and services. For nearly 145 years, ITU has coordinated the shared global use of the radio spectrum, promoted international cooperation in assigning satellite orbits, worked to improve telecommunication infrastructure in the developing world, established the worldwide standards that foster seamless interconnection of a vast range of communications systems and addressed the global challenges of our times, such as mitigating climate change and strengthening cybersecurity. Retrieved from http://www.itu.int/en/pages/default.aspx

large quantities of operational field data for monitoring. Computer technology has now been a feature of NGO head offices, where it has assisted with accounting systems and processing of field data on various aspects of NGO management systems. However, many people in the organization who collect and process other forms of data remain unclear of its value and purpose, and computer access is quite tightly controlled within the hierarchical social relations which exist in the organization. Such technology has also played a strong symbolic role within the organization, where it sends a strong message of professionalism and competence to government and funders (in contrast to many NGOs that stress informality and a grassroots focus). Far less attention is given to the critical analysis of available data for the purposes of action and learning. As Powell (2003) explains, "even with the best-constructed information has no value if it is not used. It is the flow and exchange of information which help create its value" (p.12).

With the growing importance of civil society organizations (CSOs) in development work and their prominence as important constituents in any society along with businesses and governmental organizations, the geographical diversity of CSOs thus requires efficient communication methodologies to optimize operations. With the evolution of North-South collaboration (defined by the flow of development resources and support from the northern countries to the countries in the south) (Warkentin, 2001), CSOs are becoming even more quite diverse in their compositions and operations. The North-South collaboration has redefined the scope of NGOs in the developing world with international nongovernmental organizations (INGOs) building relationships with local partners. National economies no longer remain as insulated spaces and have become very interdependent processes of production, exchange, circulation and consumption are all interlinked (Barghava & Acharya, 2008).

Having a good set of ICT and OCL tools is therefore critical for what has become today of NGO activities in many remote parts of the world as transnational CSOs or INGOs. The increasing ability of the Internet to provide multimedia access may provide opportunities and is likely to make NGOs more interactive. Moreover, the continuing global tendency towards the free flow of business and monetary infusions across nations which describes *globalization* has brought a remarkable change in significance of INGOs as they move to centre-stage in international development work in areas such as poverty alleviation, sustainable development, human rights and women's emancipation (Madon, 2000). Some INGOs (such as Oxfam, Action Aid and Save the Children) are big, complex and multi-layered systems and have their headquarters in high-income countries they receive funding from but work for the benefit of the poor in low-income countries.

The reality of dismal performance of the public sector in developing countries has led to a search for more effective organizational forms for the delivery of goods and services (SIDA, 2009). International government agencies and aid donors have focused on the efficient delivery of goods and services and making aid effective in these least developed countries (LDCs). Since the 1980s, INGOs have been instrumental in influencing global policy and have taken on a more important and substantive role in informal and formal aspects of international developmental and environmental politics (SIDA, 2009). INGOs have become synonymous with a particular style of action that has made them well known in transnational campaign networks. Though diverse in scope, interest and size, these third-generation international nongovernmental organizations have become formidable constituents in facilitating sustainable changes through international advocacy. These third generation INGOs are, in other words, dealing with a number of current development crises which require them facing up to the challenge of democratization—with calls for a more people-centered development practice and emphasis on the need to strengthen institutional capacity, supportive of greater local control, accountability, initiative and self-reliance. The types of pro-development reform involve complex organizational changes that the large official donors have little capability to address. The central leadership roles are thus assumed by organizations with potential to serve as catalysts of institutional and policy change. This means they are engaged in the strategic utilization of existing possibilities to participate with less direct involvement at grassroots level, while maximizing their influence and minimizing the risk of cooptation by maintaining established institutional links with a variety of other actors at local level (SIDA, 2009). These agencies work with poor communities through participatory methods, particularly through the action of the rapidly growing numbers of grassroots organizations (GROs) in developing countries. The successful roles of INGOs towards development work in developing countries are mainly due to their coordinated attachment to local places and cultures on the one hand and their critical engagement with global institutions in the high-income countries they are based on the other.

There is a growing informational empowerment among geographically dispersed GROs and INGOs which derive their strength from the commitment and energy of activists world-wide taking a larger role in world politics (Madon, 2000). ICTs are becoming more and more important and have been linked to successful democratic uprisings and are seen to provide information to stimulate the co-ordination of locally based activism (Allison, 2002).

Among all developing regions of the world, Africa stands out as the least networked (Department of Economic and Social Affairs, 2006). Among the reasons often discussed why Africa is so under-connected include the continent's history of colonialism until recent times, poor physical and human infrastructures, patterns of communication tied to colonial powers rather than being intra-African, large distances, and absence of a tradition of stable government. Internet usage for Africa in 2009 according to Internet Usage and World Population Statistics[9] is a minute 16% assessed from an estimated population of 1.1 billion; compared to 28% usage by Asian countries. The table on page 32 provides statistics on the Internet's big picture with respect to the various world regions.

9　Internet World Stats is an International website that features up to date world Internet Usage, Population Statistics and Internet Market Research Data, for over 233 individual countries and world regions. Internet World Stats is a useful resource for online international market research, containing the latest Internet statistics, broadband and penetration data, world population statistics and telecommunications markets information and reports. Retrieved from http://www.internetworldstats.com/

To develop—like China, a country where the Internet's potential has grown fast since the country's first connection to the Internet in 1993 with proliferation of domains and Web sites, while growing millions access the Internet from personal computers at home and the office (South China Morning Post, 1995)—the inferior state of African networking compared with the rest of the world has to be acknowledged within Africa, and steps taken to rectify the situation. Grassroots efforts to organize public networks are, however, encouraging. The creation of the African Internet Forum also testifies to the interest of the international donor community in helping to create a community of practice in Africa, and bilateral initiatives such as the USAID's Leland initiative[10] provide concrete evidence that some international assistance is happening. United Nations Economic Commission for Africa (ECA's) Enhanced Knowledge Sharing Project, promoting PRS and MDGs in Africa is another important work worthy of note. This project builds on the activities of the ECA-initiated African Learning Group on the Poverty Reduction Strategy Papers (PRSP-LG) [11], established in 2000.

---

10   The USAID Leland Initiative is a five-year, $15 million U.S. government effort to extend full Internet connectivity to 20 or more African countries. The Leland Initiative builds on existing capacity with the ultimate aim of facilitating Internet access throughout each country. Retrieved from http://www.usaid.gov/leland/

11   The Knowledge Sharing Project (KSP) on Poverty Reduction Strategies and Millennium Development Goals is an ECA-initiated project started in 2005, with support from the United Nations Department of Economic and Social Affairs (DESA). It is a direct product of a series of meetings of the African Learning Group on Poverty Reduction Strategy Papers (PRSP-LG), established in 1999 to provide a forum for the exchange of views and articulation of an African position on the Poverty Reduction Strategy Paper (PRSPs). Retrieved from http://www.knowledge.africa-devnet.org

WORLD INTERNET USAGE AND POPULATION STATISTICS - June 2012

World Regions	Population (2012 Est.)	Internet Users Dec. 31, 2000	Internet Users Latest Data	Penetration (% Popula-tion)	Growth 2000-2012	Users % of Table
Africa	1,073,380,925	4,514,400	167,335,676	16 %	3,600 %	7.0 %
Asia	3,922,066,987	114,304,000	1,076,681,059	28 %	840 %	44.8 %
Europe	820,918,446	105,096,093	518,512,109	63 %	390 %	21.5 %
Middle East	223,608,203	3,284,800	90,000,455	40 %	2,640 %	3.7 %
North America	348,280,154	108,096,800	273,785,413	79 %	150 %	11.4 %
Latin America / Caribbean	593,688,638	18,068,919	254,915,745	43 %	1,310 %	10.6 %
Oceania / Austra-lia	35,903,569	7,620,480	24,287,919	68 %	220 %	1.0 %
World Total	7,017,846,922	360,985,492	2,405,518,376	34 %	566 %	100.0 %

Note: Retrieved from "Internet World Stats" by Miniwatts Marketing Group, http://www.internetworldstats.com

The PRSP-LG is a forum for African peer learning and information sharing on the PRSP experience within the continent. The project is developing electronically enhanced mechanisms for ongoing interactive knowledge sharing and peer learning on national strategies for growth and poverty reduction in Africa. The project currently maintains a Community of Practice (CoP) discussion platform—a virtual network of practitioners sharing knowledge, experiences and skills in the areas of poverty reduction and MDGs.

Also, Afrik-IT listserv[12] continues to facilitate information technology development in Africa; and a similar role is played by S-Asia-IT[13] which seeks to help expand the impact of Internet initiatives and enhance coordination among development actors in South Asia. IT professionals, Internet service providers, international agencies, and non-governmental organizations (NGOs), educators, activists and all others interested in IT are encouraged to get involved. S-Asia-IT is hosted by Asia Pacific Network Information Centre (APNIC)[14].

12　CataList is the official catalog of public LISTSERV® lists. It allows you to browse and search for mailing lists of interest and get information about LISTSERV host sites. African Network of IT Experts and Professionals (ANITEP) List/Afrik-IT listserv is listed in Catalist.
Retrieved from https://listserv.heanet.ie/cgi-bin/wa?INDEX&X=&Y=

13　S-Asia-IT, a mailing/discussion list for IT developments in South Asia—Bangladesh, Bhutan, India, Maldives, Nepal, Pakistan, and Sri Lanka—is intended to provide a forum for those interested in the development and use of information technology in the South Asian context. Our specific interest is in advancing information technologies to support equitable social and economic development in the region, recognizing that the development of information and communication technologies, particularly internet connectivity, are important tools in this work by activists, donors, NGOs, government and the private sector. Retrieved from http://mailman.apnic.net/mailman/listinfo/s-asia-it

14　The Asia Pacific Network Information Center (APNIC) is the Regional Internet Registry for the Asia Pacific Region. APNIC provides number resource allocation and registration services that support the global operation of the Internet. It is a not-for-profit, membership-based organization whose members include Internet Service Providers, National Internet Registries, and similar organizations.
Retrieved from http://www.apnic.net/

Again, using the Internet strategically is demonstrated with the development and operation of a global computer network for non-governmental organizations (NGOs)—the Association for Progressive Communications (APC)[15], which grew from a global network of NGOs and Internet service providers that began in the 1980s. Today, APC co-ordinates existing NGO networks electronically, provides access to 20,000 activists in 133 countries around the world making systematic use of information systems in both ICT-based and non-ICT based to debate issues such as war prevention, protection of the environment, human rights and democracy—thus providing an information sharing network on international cooperation.

ICT networking tools appear to amplify social collaboration made simple as cohorts are connected by fax and email with computers serving as catalysts and providing the means for people to readily interact. There has been much information sharing by NGOs and their use of ICTs show that these organizations make frequent use of phone-, fax- and modem-based communication systems. NGOs have also begun to reach out through informal education networks. NGO operators are utilizing traditional communication skills to describe problems and requirements of poor urban slum dwellers and rural communities through audiocassettes and video tapes messaging. For example, in Thailand, community learning centers (CLCs) have been established to serve as a focal point for providing non-formal and informal education activities for local people with the support of the German Adult Education Association dvv international.[16] In this context, the use of ICT

---

15   The Association for Progressive Communications (APC) is an international network of civil society organizations dedicated to empowering and supporting groups and individuals working for peace, human rights, development and protection of the environment, through the strategic use of information and communication technologies (ICTs), including the internet.
Retrieved from http://old.apc.org/english/index.shtml

16   dvv international promotes development through cooperation in youth and adult education. dvv international is the Institute for International Cooperation of the German Adult Education Association (Deutscher Volkshochschul-Verband.e,V., DVV) which, in turn, is the federal umbrella

tools for development implies knowing what local initiative is essential for the appropriate integration of information technology mechanisms into communities.

Social identities of OCL

NGOs' use of communication methodologies in civil society interventions underscores the multi-institutional dynamics of civil society development and how they are working cooperatively, leveraging each other's unique contributions to achieve greater efficiency, innovation, impact, scale and/or sustainability. Collaboration facilitates the sharing of multiple perspectives. In OCL, collaboration has been defined as a process where all who are involved in the process are active participants in the communicative process, where knowledge is something that emerges from active dialog (Beaudin, 1999).

NGOs can benefit from the asynchronous collaboration capabilities of OCL with the potential for increased participant interaction. OCL's asynchronous capabilities combined with the written record are of a communicative type not possible in verbal conversations (Harasim, *et. al.*, 1995). In online collaboration, reflection and interaction are linked, a group can resolve multiple ideas concomitantly, and improvements in conversational balance, equality and consensus are possible (Roberts, 2004). Collaboration is therefore an aid to education and facilitates the formation of a virtual learning community (Schuler, 1996).

Collaborative learning produces the distinctive learning environment that supports beneficial information exchange, trust building, sharing of ideas, and ongoing collaborative processes. Learners work together

---

association for the 16 regional associations of Germany's community adult education centers. The domestic and international work of dvv international is guided by a commitment to human rights and the Institute's principles on the promotion of women and gender equality. dvv international is active on a worldwide basis, cooperating with more than 200 partners in over 30 countries. Retrieved from http://www.iiz-dvv.de/

in participation. They form "learning communities" that are productive. Collaboration by ICTs thus supports the building of archetypical online learning communities that connect participants globally (Mele, 1999). These online communities could be global and rather disparate in numbers and objectives, and even linguistically, culturally, academically; yet share common interests and self-regulation, informal ties and community identification. The governing processes within these virtual communities are collaboration through many-to-many communication, convictions, and information and knowledge sharing. Among NGOs, such collaboration offers great potential for improving methodological participation as well as testing concepts and exploring development assumptions. The use of OCL technologies is therefore a form of social learning as an appropriate process for change.

Over the years, the OCL concept has been explored in a number of ways. Information technologists focused initially on web portals (Cairncros, 1997) and rapid technological innovation (Gurstein, 2000) which was greatly accelerated by digital tools that now make it possible to access text, audio, visual and database information in an interactive environment (Hamelink, 1997.

However, it is important to note that, irrespective of the way the concept has been explored, almost all OCL research conceptualizes online collaborative learning primarily as essential to an organizations' capacity for growth and central to the management of any project. The essence of online collaboration is analysis of the technological processes and the structuring of the requisite online platforms (Tomei, 2009). However, there is little emphasis on the mechanics of web based interactivity, i.e. the coordination of the movement of information among organizational users. These mechanics of web-based interactivity thus speaks to the social identity theory of online collaborative learning that draws on and integrates broadly conceived principles of social identity theory (Smith & Lipsky, 1993). Social identity is a unifying construct for OCL processes. The impact on the social context and social identity of OCL usage by nongovernmental organizations can be seen in online communities involved in discussions of topical issues ranging from issues about the environment, good governance, and corruption. The social identities of OCL also recognize the simultaneous development of interactive technology and nongovernmental organizations which are faced with a growing necessity to promote innovation in order to move toward a more integrated role in nongovernmental work (Mele, 1999). Key concepts such as cohesion, participation, accountability and organizational norms are theoretically the social identity constructs of OCL. Design features that 'collectivize' rather than 'personalize' OCL can promote psychological issues that are crucial for successful collaborations (i.e. group cohesion, accountability to the organization, and increased participation, and norms for success) are generally recognized as integral features of successful collaboration and are key variables for increasing productivity in organizations.

Development NGOs can therefore work toward empowering their pro-development functions by seeking ways to increase their impact effectiveness and overall professionalism. This should lead them to recognize the importance of the types of information systems required for their operation and activities. There is the need for information about their work on the ground which is crucial to ensure the social identity constructs of group cohesion, accountability, to learn from experience and to develop and disseminate good practice. There is also the need to gain access to information about wider contextual forces such as macro-economic policy, the national and local political climate, and the ongoing work of other organizational actors. This type of contextual information is increasingly important for development NGOs if they are to campaign for policy changes at national and international levels.

Each and every one of us has the power to leave this world a better place than we found it. But we would argue that we do so not by creating grandiose plans, or imagining ourselves as some part of a vast movement, but by the small day-to-day actions and decisions that together with the actions of millions of others, can transform the world.

Linda Kaplan Thaler

Chapter 2: The 'Digital Divide' and its challenges for developing countries

The potential of ICTs to improve the livelihood of people and contribute to human development does suggest impressive outcomes. Being that human development is a process of enlarging people's choices, when like-minded people can cooperate across great distances to defend human rights or promote other projects of common interests, the benefits are phenomenal. However, there are obvious challenges with this development over digital technologies. With a world economy that is already polarized, the convergence of the digital advantage in regions where the information infrastructure is quite developed means the developing regions (regions that are not endowed with the most modern capabilities) must really orient themselves to take advantage of the information economy.

The spread of Internet in developing nations is presented by some as dangerously widening the existing differences between the poor and the rich in these regions (Meyer, 1997). Already today these gaps are greater in developing countries than in industrial nations. A clear incidence of such widening gap is the "software forge" in India (D'Costa & Sridharan, 2004) and the transfer of jobs from Northern countries to the South. But the example of India demonstrates that this fact isn't combined with improvement for all Indian people. Even though the United Nations Conference on Trade and Development (UNCTAD) has credited India with a projected economic growth of 8.1%—quite a faster rate of expansion in the world after China, nevertheless, India remains a country of stark contrasts—as home to the largest rural-urban disparities in the world, with its development index ranked at 119 out of 169 countries. Financing affordable Internet access and ICT competence including investment and training to create, maintain, and expand computer networks remains a challenge in India as is the case in many other developing countries in South Asia. The major implication is to keep up and indeed sustain the commitment to equity, so that the Internet does not become a major engine of global inequality. Conclusions in a recent

World Bank study (2011) show that the technology gap between the rich OECD countries and the non-OECD nations remains huge, and growing. Moreover, the growing ICT gap and the ever-increasing wealth gap are considered to be mutually reinforcing with noxious implications for political and commercial relations among nations, as well as for political dynamics within nations (Wilson, 1999).

The promise of using the Internet to benefit the greater majority and vulnerable groups in particular are considered within the broader framework of actual needs and existing facilities of Third World communities. The digital revolution offers developing countries unique opportunities, allowing less-developed countries to 'leapfrog' over costly stages of development and catch up with more developed countries. But in most developing countries, nonetheless, telecommunications infrastructure has long been neglected. The realities of civil wars, hunger, malnutrition, diseases, lack of jobs, and unequal distribution of income in Third World countries are more important challenges. As a result, the telecommunications infrastructure is critically underdeveloped, and the cost of using it is generally more expensive in developing countries than in developed ones. The key measures of telecommunications access being 'tele-density'; as tele-density[17] stands today, the average number of main telephone lines per 100 people is a mere 1.12 in heavily indebted poor countries (HIPC) the world's poorest countries, as opposed to 57 in the richest ones, according to a World Bank report. (WDI, 2012). In addition to a lack of wire-line telephone services, the poor electric-

---

17   In earlier days, 'tele-density' was computed as the number of fixed telephone lines per hundred inhabitants. But this method has become less significant with an increasing number of countries register a trend of mobile cellular subscribers outnumbering the fixed line connections. Hence, as an alternative, 'mobi-density' or mobile cellular subscribers per hundred inhabitants was proposed. Since this method is a disadvantage for to some countries where the fixed line network is well established, or others where the mobile network is still in its initial stage of development, 'effective tele-density' has been proposed by the International telecommunication Union (ITU) as the solution, which is defined as either fixed line connections or mobile subscribers per hundred inhabitants—whichever is higher. (ITU, 2010).

ity supply infrastructure, especially in rural and remote areas, has an impact in many ways. In accordance with data from the World Bank the costs for one telephone connection in inner-city regions of the Third World is about 500 to 1,500 United States dollars. The ITU's objective to connect a thousand persons with ten telephone mainlines in Sub-Saharan Africa would consume 28 billion dollars. Developing countries already have a foreign debt burden of billions of dollars.

The widening knowledge gap between the developed and developing countries is being further aggravated by the widening rifts between these wired societies—known as the 'Digital Divide'. The 'Digital Divide' holds ominous consequences for employment levels, under-development and poverty in developing countries. Critical infrastructure assets, including international and local links are inadequate and not reliable; equipment is difficult to obtain, maintain, and repair.

There are difficulties in harnessing an unbiased and equitable system of patents and intellectual property rights that is friendly to developing poor countries in Sub-Saharan Africa. The existing systems limit access to certain services and materials and need expensive modern technologies in order to be accessed. More so, triangulation of research data from different regions is difficult and many times impossible hence preventing holism in intervention designs for fighting poverty or the replicability of positive development practices in other parts of Sub-Saharan Africa especially areas cut-off from major ICTs like mobile telephone and internet services. Besides, minimal ICTs have affected an enabling environment for market entries and marred the movement of heavy cash flows needed in most Foreign Direct Investments. Financial transactions are too slow and have led to stakeholders preferring other areas like Asia and Latin America for investments than Sub-Saharan Africa.

Also, the architecture in terms of computing hardware and connections, or software framework and protocols, requires skills to establish and operate. Knowledge of network administration and network design—including local area and wide area networks—is required. Knowledge of how to establish network services and serve information over the net, regardless of subject matter, is required. Quantifiable and comparative measures to broader context of the social and the cultural milieu within a country remain important in understanding how those skills are generated and used. Responsiveness to knowledge production in modern scientific knowledge, the strength of the work ethic, and attitudes and policies toward efficiency and effectiveness in the achievement of objectives all are important in the successful generation and accumulation of knowledge. In general, within developing country environments, such specialized knowledge and links to multinationals are in short supply. Data on brain drain in developing regions of the world show a continent losing the very people—the scarce, more talented individuals—it needs most for economic, social, scientific, and technological progress (Docquier & Rapoport, 2007).

Moreover, while it may be true that certain development problems can be resolved through technological 'leap-frogging' without having to rise through the traditional stages of development, it is also true that access to such solutions presupposes a relatively high level of development, which many developing countries simply do not have (Chonia, 2002).

The use of computer communications by NGOs for networking, education and social justice

The use of computer communications by NGOs for networking, education and social justice goes to show that the advancement of ICTs has an intra-organizational dimension—it is socially formed, socially configured and socially enacted. ICTs are the support systems for OCLs, they are mutated in electronic interaction, and their expression in discourse and action is framed by the social context. OCL is grounded in social consensus defined by the organizational mandate—many, if not most, of OCL activities reflect and even define the organization that participating operators belong to or identify with. OCL phenomena are impacted significantly by social identity processes—they are socially structured and grounded in social consensus, organizational constituents and social identities (Kahn, 2000).

OCL is placed within a more elaborated analysis of the social context, a context in which socio-historical, socio-structural, and ideological factors impact upon the formation, stability, and outcomes of OCL activities. The unprecedented revolution of NGOs and their potential for developing their innovative capacity is linked to their use of interactive technology (Gurstein, 2000). Clearly, there is a move away by NGOs from information brokering toward the facilitation of knowledge networks. Much of this impetus for NGO activity growth may allow the unfolding of innovative capacity, but it also raises accountability issues and questions about the future form and function of NGOs (Gurstein, 2000).

OCL has the advantage of interactive tools used as aid to collaborative learning. These applications have evolved from years of hard work, inspired by research on various market driven software packages. Online collaboration and interactivity is effective with computer-mediated communication (CMC) tools which support any forms of communicative transaction that occur through the use of two or more networked computers. While CMC has traditionally referred to those communications that occur via computer-mediated formats (e.g. bulletin boards, instant messaging, email, chat rooms), it is applicable to other forms of asynchronous structure text-based transactions such as text messaging, and computer video conferencing as well as access to information, e.g. the use of online databases. Research on CMC focuses largely on the social effects of different computer-supported communication technologies. Many recent studies involve Internet-based social networking supported by social software resourcefully used to promote activist programs of certain NGOs, for e.g. the broadcasting of human rights violations in many places where these violations occur. Use of e-mail, Twitter, YouTube computer-mediated formats in disseminating evidences of violations across borders has generated appropriate international action against such violations. Human rights groups such as Amnesty International, Human Rights Watch, Washington Office on Latin America (WOLA), *Centro de Documentacion e Informacion sobre Derechos Humanos en America Latina*, Inter-African Network for Human Rights and Development, and many others are using the

Internet for advocacy to inform about human rights issues. The 1989 Tianamen Square Massacre (Miller, Vandome, & McBrewster, 2009) in Beijing, the excesses of the 1991 xenophobic riots against foreigners in Germany (Bade & Anderson, 1994), the conflict of Chiapas between Zapatistas and the Mexican government that started in 1994, the publication of the declarations of the Ejército Zapatista de Liberación Nacional (EZLN) by the Mexican newspaper La Jornada, the unfortunate case of Ken Saro-Wiwa[18] in Nigeria were all instances where the Internet played a crucial role in bringing them to the world.

The evolution of the Internet has thus created these many possibilities and there is no dearth in resources to empower NGOs. NGOs and civil society organizations (CSOs) with which they work, including grassroots and village organizations, associations and other citizens' groups, are key agents of change for Africa's social and economic development, but all too often their management and technology resources fall short of their expertise in information and communication technology for development. At the 2008 African ICT Best Practices Forum in Burkina

---

18   Kenule "Ken" Beeson Saro Wiwa (October 10, 1941 – November 10, 1995) was a Nigerian author, television producer, environmental activist, and winner of the Goldman Environmental Prize. Ken Saro-Wiwa was a member of the Ogoni people, an ethnic minority in Nigeria whose homeland, Ogoniland, in the Niger Delta has been targeted for crude oil extraction since the 1950s and which has suffered extreme and unremediated environmental damage from decades of indiscriminate petroleum waste dumping. Initially as spokesperson, and then as President, of the Movement for the Survival of the Ogoni People (MOSOP), Saro-Wiwa led a nonviolent campaign against environmental degradation of the land and waters of Ogoniland by the operations of the multinational petroleum industry, especially the Royal Dutch Shell Company. He was also an outspoken critic of the Nigerian government, which he viewed as reluctant to enforce environmental regulations on the foreign petroleum companies operating in the area. At the peak of his nonviolent campaign, Saro-Wiwa was arrested, hastily tried by a special military tribunal, and hanged in 1995 by the military government of General Sani Abacha, all on charges widely viewed as entirely politically motivated and completely unfounded. His execution provoked international outrage and resulted in Nigeria's suspension from the Commonwealth of Nations for over three years. Source: Genocide in Nigeria – The Ogoni Tragedy.

Faso, Microsoft Corp expanded its commitment to NGOs with a new skills training and support program called the NGO Information and Communication Technology for Development (ICT4D) Academy. The NGO ICT4D Academy focuses on three areas critical to each NGO's regional scalability and long-term sustainability: ICT4D skills development, IT support services and e-Readiness. Key partners, including the Aga Khan Foundation and the Academy for Educational Development, support the NGO ICT4D Academy's effort to enable NGOs across Africa in integrating traditional and ICT methods as tools for development.

Chapter 3: OCL digital possibilities

Electronic mail (e-mail) has been one of the oldest and most successful of asynchronous collaborative tools (Gilbert, 1994). The e-mail supports a broader range of activities including the possibilities of many-to-many communication functionality such as e-mail discussion lists which provide even broader possibilities NGO operators can use to advance advocacy. E-mail is usually available in every OCL and today most participants in Internet usage have one or more e-mail accounts. However, some limitations of the e-mail often discussed point to its lack of organization and the likelihood of information overload occurring when multiple topics or large groups are involved. However, notwithstanding its limitations, the e-mail remains an excellent tool for communicating private information and working on collaborative projects involving small group sizes.

The *e-forum* is a collaborative tool as a public conference of participants. Discussions in such forums are transcripts in easily accessible formats. E-forums use related conversational items (commonly called discussion threads) with many advantages and can be organized by subject, group, or other criteria (Anderson & Hanuka, 1997). NGOS can make effective use of e-forums in projects development. Having a good set of tools is critical to online collaborative learning. OCL can facilitate a strong sense of community and some basic knowledge about stakeholders in projects typical in face-to-face environments. In these online communities there are ongoing discussions that stimulate collaborative learning. Ideally, anyone can start a discussion and people from different walks of life are encouraged to participate, optimally creating various discussion threads on topical issues ranging from issues about the environment, good governance, corruption, etc. Such interactions stimulate active learning.

Further, the touch points of meaningful inquiry in a wired world have inspired exploration with new digital projects and tools.

- iCohere[19] conference tools offer all kinds of possibilities with online conferences. Keynote addresses, breakout sessions, exhibit halls—even happ-E hours are brought to attendees online. The program integrates webinars, streaming video and audio, discussion boards with RSS, file libraries and vendor showrooms.

- GoPetition[20] is a petition writing tool that is used as a flexible campaign tool and dynamic software designed for campaigners to report success stories.

- Avaaz[21] is a transnational online community that empowers millions of people from all walks of life to take action on pressing global, regional and national

---

19   iCohere is an affordable, highly configurable collaboration platform for online events and professional communities. Since 2001, the iCohere team has been an innovator in online learning, knowledge communities and large-scale online events. Beyond technology, we offer facilitation strategies, action plans and consulting services to help you create valuable online communities. Retrieved from http://www.icohere.com/

20   GoPetition – a leading international petition hosting portal – offers advanced global hosting services and unrivalled customer service. Ranked # 1 by Google for petition writing, GoPetition has over 30,000 petitions in more than 75 countries. GoPetition has helped many campaigners achieve success stories and has developed an international presence with broad support from the world community. GoPetition is a non-partisan site and has no political affiliations. Our aim is to provide access to quality software and tailored petition hosting services. Our customer service goal is to maintain same-day service standards. All petitions at GoPetition are instantly available when uploaded.
Retrieved from http://www.gopetition.com/

21   Avaaz—meaning "voice" in several European, Middle Eastern and Asian languages—launched in 2007 with a simple democratic mission: to organize citizens of all nations to close the gap between the world we have and the world most people everywhere want. The Avaaz community campaigns in 15 languages served by a core team on 6 continents and thousands of volunteers. Avaaz takes action—signing petitions, funding media campaigns and direct actions, emailing, calling and lobbying governments, and organizing "offline" protests and events—to ensure that the views and values of the world's people inform the decisions that affect us all. Retrieved from http://www.avaaz.org

issues—from corruption and poverty to conflict and climate change.

- Video blogs[22] and Podcasts[23] are also tools growing in popularity in many developing countries.

- CPsquare[24] member's blogs feed for communities of practice is like a town square, a place where people gather to connect and learn together.

- Netsquared[25] enables social benefit organizations to leverage the tools of the social web.

- YouNoodle[26] develops innovative ways to bring together the information, people and technology that help start-ups succeed.

- Doodle[27] eliminates the chaos of scheduling and saves users a lot of time and energy when trying to find a

---

22   See Associated Content web pages for more content material on video blogging tools. Retrieved from http://www.associatedcontent.com/article/1166625/video_blogging_tools_and_video_blog.html?cat=15

23   See Podcast Alley featuring the best Podcast directory. Retrieved from http://www.podcastalley.com/

24   See Cpsquare website for more details at http://cpsquare.org/

25   NetSquared is focused on the intersection of technology and social impact. NetSquared creates opportunities for all those involved in creating change to connect. Retrieved from http://www.netsquared.org/

26   YouNoodle provides a platform for so far 50 of the world's top university entrepreneurship clubs and competitions, serving tens of thousands of members and thousands of startups. YouNoodle tools help to effectively manage business competitions, events, mailing lists and community development. Startup Predictor is the first in a series of decision-making tools YouNoodle plans to introduce for the startup industry. YouNoodle's development team studied thousands of current and past startups, using both publicly available and proprietary data, to determine patterns of predictive factors for early-stage companies' success. YouNoodle is based in San Francisco, California. Retrieved from http://www.younoodle.com/

27   Instead of using just one option, Doodle enables users to propose several dates and times and the participants can indicate their availability online. Participants will find the perfect time to meet in a quick and easy way no matter how many people and calendars are involved. Doodle is free

time to bring a number of people together. The service is used for business and personal scheduling by more than 10 million people per month.

- JustMeans[28] provides a platform for learning about the ideas, companies, and people shaping the world of corporate social responsibility (CSR), sustainability, and social enterprise.

- QuickBooks[29] Online accounting software is designed to be easy to use for small business accounting, yet powerful enough for experienced online accounting professionals. Online accounting software is web-based, so users can use it anywhere there is Internet access. QuickBooks Online accounting software lets users track sales, create invoices, and monitor expenses. And by adding in online banking, online payroll, and time tracking capabilities, financial management features in QuickBooks Online are even more robust.

- Professional Article Writing Software[30] products are incredibly user-friendly and uncomplicated for NGO

---

and doesn't require registration. Advanced users can connect their calendars, customize their own Doodle, and use a lot of extra features. Doodle offers scheduling for everyone. Retrieved from http://www.doodle.com/

28   JustMeans is a platform for connecting businesses that are socially responsible with users that appreciate being informed not only about a company's ethics, but what a company is doing to insure that they are upholding the standards they have set and obligations they have committed to from a social standpoint. JustMeans is not only a network to help introduce businesses to social media, but a platform for collective social change. Retrieved from http://www.justmeans.com/

29   QuickBooks Online Accounting Software provides easy-to-use online accounting software for small businesses. It's a simple, feature-rich online version of America's most popular accounting software. Retrieved from http://quickbooksonline.intuit.com/

30   Some articles writing software products include ContentFX (http://wwwcontentfx.com/video.php/); Articleapps (http://www.articleapps.com/index.php/); SimplyPLR (http://www.simplyplr.com/); and Instant Article Wizard (http://www.instantarticlewizard.com).

professionals to use to generate specialized content material on just about any subject matter working with a content generator. One can therefore create search engine optimization (SEO) content loaded articles or blog posts with the aid of a professional writer software.

There are many other online resources that offer suggestions especially tailored to setting up and maintaining community ICT and networking projects, including community technology centers (tele-centers). Some sites also offer tips for activities at such centers, such as how to work with diverse populations and how to build on shared resources for development.

- Development in Practice[31] is an online journal that offers practice-relevant analysis and research relating to development and humanitarianism, providing a worldwide forum for the exchange of ideas and practical experiences among practitioners, scholars, policy shapers, and activists.

- *@ Ease with E-mail*[32] is a handbook on using electronic mail for NGOs in developing countries—a tool developed by the United Nations Non-Governmental Liaison Service (UN-NGLS) and the Friedrich Ebert Foundation (New York office).

---

31 'Development in Practice' is a hybrid Open Access journal that seeks to stimulate new thinking and ways of working. Contributors to this peer-reviewed journal represent a wide range of cultural and professional backgrounds and experience. While the journal is published in English, submissions in French, Portuguese or Spanish are welcome; and abstracts are published in these languages. *Development in Practice* particularly encourages new writers as well as previously published authors. Retrieved from http://www.developmentinpractice.org/

32 @ Ease with Email is designed to explain basic terms and concepts, offers advice and contacts, lists existing computer communications networks and local e-mail service providers in developing countries, and suggests ways to benefit from these communication tools. Retrieved from http://www.unsystem.org/ngls/documents/publications.en/email/index.htm

- Bridges.Org[33] International Digital Divide Resources provides a database of educational materials and curricula and appropriate technology guides, e-readiness assessment tools, information about "*e-democracy*," and a listing of regional digital divide resources.

- LINGOs (Learning for International Non-Governmental Organizations)[34] works to improve the performance, and lower the cost and increase the effectiveness of Non-Governmental Organizations (NGOs).

- Bellanet[35] promotes and facilitates effective collaboration within the international community, especially through the use of ICTs. Bellanet supports effective

---

33   Bridges.org is an international organization with a mission to promote the effective use of information and communications technology (ICT) in the developing world for meaningful purposes, such as better healthcare, education and self-sustaining economic development. Bridges.org seeks to bring a practical vision to the realities of ICT-enabled socio-economic development, and an important aspect of its strategy is to apply basic business principles and processes in development projects. Bridges.org conducts technology research, evaluations and policy analysis to inform civil society organizations, governments, development aid agencies and the business community and help them improve the way they integrate ICT into their activities. This in turn brings the benefits of technology to more people— students, small business owners, doctors and their patients and the general public—in more meaningful ways: not only to overcome the challenges and adversities they face, but to give them the tools to build their own solutions and manage their own affairs in more efficient ways. Retrieved from http://www.bridges.org/

34   LINGOs is a consortium of over 45 international humanitarian relief, development, conservation and health organizations. LINGOs provides the latest learning technologies and courses from our partners so these nonprofits can increase the skill levels of their employees, and therefore increasing the impact of their programs. Retrieved from http://ngolearning.org/default.aspx

35   Bellanet.com offers secure ColdFusion MX web hosting on Windows 2003 Servers. With Domain Name Registration, SSL Certificate Registration, IMail E-Mail Servers and FTP Servers, BellaNet.com can provide its users with everything they need to get up and running. Retrieved from http://www.bellanet.com/

development practice by sharing its expertise in information and communication technologies as well as its skills in facilitating organizational learning and the sharing of knowledge.

- Oneworldgroup.org[36] is the human rights and development site aggregator that pioneers Internet and mobile phone applications that the world's poorest people can use to improve their life chances, and that help people everywhere understand global problems—and do something about them.

- Capacity.org[37] is a web magazine-cum-portal intended for practitioners and policy makers who work in or on capacity development in international cooperation in the South.

- ALNAP (Active Learning Network for Accountability and Performance in Humanitarian Action)[38] is an

---

36   At Oneworldgroup.org, live editors categorize information which is formatted as the OneWorld entry point for those seeking access to the human rights and development sector on the Web. Oneworldgroup.org has a variety of interactive tools that foster communities. Retrieved from http://www.oneworldgroup.org/

37   Capacity.org is a web magazine-cum-portal intended for practitioners and policy makers who work in or on capacity development in international cooperation in the South. The site is accompanied by a printed journal and an email newsletter, which are published quarterly in English, French and Spanish. Each issue of Capacity.org focuses on a specific theme relevant to capacity development, with feature articles, reports on policy and practice, interviews and a guest column, and annotated links to related web resources, publications and events. Retrieved from http://www.capacity.org/

38   The Active Learning Network for Accountability and Performance in Humanitarian Action (ALNAP) was established in 1997, following the multi-agency evaluation of the Rwanda genocide. ALNAP is a collective response by the humanitarian sector, dedicated to improving humanitarian performance through increased learning and accountability. A unique network, ALNAP incorporates many of the key humanitarian organizations and experts from across the humanitarian sector. Members are drawn from donors, NGOs, the Red Cross/Crescent, the UN, independents and aca-

international inter-agency forum with an active-learning membership network, dedicated to improving the quality and accountability of humanitarian action, by sharing lessons; identifying common problems; and where appropriate, building consensus on approaches.

- *Free*Lists[39] provides free mailing list hosting to groups whose topics are related to technology, computers, communications, medicine, astronomy, etc.

- Capaciteria[40] is a free service designed to help nonprofits find the best resources to build their institutional capacity.

- Gust[41] provides the global platform for the sourcing and management of early-stage investments.

---

demics. ALNAP uses the broad range of experience and expertise within its membership to produce tools and analysis relevant and accessible to the humanitarian sector as a whole. Retrieved from http://www.alnap.org/

39   *Free*Lists provides free mailing list hosting to groups whose topics are related to technology, computers, communications, medicine, astronomy, etc. *Free*Lists provides a free service to help people keep in touch with friends, customers, co-workers, research partners, and more. *Free*Lists provides the internet community with Free, no-hassle, high-quality mailing lists. Retrieved from http://www.freelists.org/

40   Nonprofit capacity support is a critical issue, and like all mission-based issues nonprofits deal with, resolving the problem has two major components. One involves tangible resourcing. The other involves useful information to help nonprofits make better decisions just as they assist their own constituencies. Capaciteria addresses the information component of the nonprofit capacity support issue by providing useful resources. Retrieved from http://www.capaciteria.org/

41   Gust enables skilled entrepreneurs to collaborate with the smartest investors by virtually supporting all aspects of the investment relationship, from initial pitch to successful exit. Gust is endorsed by the world's leading business angel and venture capital associations, and powers over 750 investment organizations in 65 countries. More than 125,000 start-ups have already used the platform to connect and collaborate with over 35,000 individual accredited investors. Retrieved from https://gust.com/

- Aspiration[42] helps nonprofits and foundations use software tools more effectively and sustainably.

- Creative Commons[43] is a nonprofit corporation dedicated to making it easier for people to share and build upon the work of others, consistent with the rules of copyright.

- Gurteen Knowledge[44] website is primarily a resource for the Gurteen Knowledge Community—a global learning community of over 17,000 people in 160 countries. The main themes of this site are knowledge management, learning, creativity, innovation and personal development and it consists of over 5,000 pages.

- Eldis Communities[45] is a free online interactive space where development professionals meet others involved

---

42   Aspiration serves as ally, coach, strategist, mentor and facilitator to those trying to make more impactful use of information technology in their social change efforts. Retrieved from http://aspirationtech.org/

43   Creative Commons provides free licenses and other legal tools to mark creative work with the freedom the creator wants it to carry, so others can share, remix, use commercially, or any combination thereof. Retrieved from http://creativecommons.org/

44   The Gurteen Knowledge community is for people who are committed to making a difference: people who wish to share and learn from each other and who strive to see the world differently, think differently and act differently. Membership of the community is diverse but members have common traits - they: are committed to making a difference, are inclined to action, see themselves as thought-leaders and change activists, recognize the importance of understanding through dialogue and conversation, have a passion for learning, are open minded and non-judgmental by nature, and value diversity and cultural differences.

45   Eldis Communities offers free membership and group creation—a service that is financially supported by the Eldis donor group. Members can join groups and network with other members of the community. Groups can be public or private, and members can select which tools they want to use (discussions, blog, file stores, calendar, and wiki). The Community is web-based, but members can also choose to receive email notifications from the site when new content is added (and can also post messages to group discussions by email). Retrieved from http://community.eldis.org/

in international development work, discuss issues that are important and share useful resources.

- ACP Business Climate Facility[46] provides technical assistance for improving the business climate in Africa, the Pacific and the Caribbean.

- DGroups[47] is a platform for groups in international development in a partnership that caters to both individuals and organizations by offering tools and services that bring people together.

- Grou.ps[48] is a do-it-yourself social networking platform that allows people to come together and form interactive communities around a shared interest or affiliation with built-in apps enabling easy collaboration and communication.

- Zunia[49] provides a space of knowledge-sharing among development practitioners worldwide. Users can access

---

46   ACP Business Climate facility provides technical assistance for improving the business climate in Africa, the Pacific and the Caribbean. Retrieved from http://bizclim.ning.com/

47   DGroups is an online platform for individuals and organizations working in international development. It is a place where individuals and organizations in the development sector can come together and interact with one another. DGroups is a joint initiative of leading international development organizations such as CTA, DFID, FAO, HIVOS, ICCO, IICD and other organizations committed to support dialogue through development. Retrieved from http://www.dgroups.org/

48   GROU.PS platform is used to create a wide variety of community sites, including online gaming forums, e-learning classrooms, fan clubs, charity fundraising campaigns, college alumni societies, and event planning portals. Any organization seeking to aggregate and organize people online can greatly improve its effectiveness, engagement and appeal by migrating to the GROU.PS platform. By giving any user the ability to create an easy-to-use, yet powerful, social network, GROU.PS is propelling online collaboration, communication and content sharing in a new socially aware direction. Retrieved from http://www.grou.ps/home/

49   Zunia provides membership that is free and open to all interested individuals. While you do not need to be a member to access information on

and post news, events, best practices and publications that are searchable online and receive e-mail alerts on topics of their interest.

- Twitter[50]is an information network that brings people closer to what is important to them.

- Facebook[51] is a hugely popular social networking service launched in February 2004, intended to connect friends, family, and business associates.

- Xing[52] is a social network that powers business professionals by giving them the tools to tap into the vast resources of their own personal network to open doors to thousands of companies, find jobs, and search for employment.

- LinkedIn[53] is the world's largest professional network with over 175 million members and rapidly growing.

Zunia, being a member has many advantages. As a member you can post news, events, publications, etc., receive customized email alerts and set up filters, create a profile, network with 60,000+ Zunia members and contact them online. Retrieved from http://www.zunia.org/

50   Every day, millions of people turn to Twitter to connect to their interests, to share information, and find out what's happening in the world in real time. Anyone can read, write and share messages of up to 140 characters on Twitter. These messages, or tweets, are available to anyone interested in reading them, whether logged in or not. This unique combination of open, public, and unfiltered tweets delivered in a simple, standardized 140 character unit allows Twitter users to share and discover what's happening on any device in real time. Retrieved from https://business.twitter.com/

51   Facebook is the largest social network in the world with over 950 million users worldwide. Basically, Facebook allows its members to communicate, connect and engage with each other, both directly and through various applications and features. Retrieved from http://www.facebook.com/

52   XING is a social software platform for business professionals. The platform offers personal profiles, groups, discussion forums, event coordination, and other social community features. Basic membership is free. But many core functions like searching for people with specific qualifications or messaging people to whom one is not already connected can only be accessed by paid premium members. Retrieved from https://www.xing.com/

53   LinkedIn (NYSE: LNKD) is a social networking website for people in

- Viadeo[54] is a business networking service, a social network for business professionals that is heavily used in Europe.
- Wikispaces[55] is a free OCL tool people are able to use to create learning communities, build new pages, post messages, and keep track of topics they are interested in.
- RSS (Rich Site Summary, most commonly expanded as "Really Simple Syndication")[56] is a format for deliver-

---

professional occupations. Founded in December 2002 and launched on May 5, 2003, LinkedIn is mainly used for professional networking. As of June 2012, LinkedIn reports more than 175 million users in more than 200 countries and territories. Retrieved from https://www.linkedin.com/

54 Viadeo is considered the second largest business networking service after LinkedIn. People who use Viadeo not only keep a profile, but also can make a list of their business partners, a connection that is little more robust than LinkedIn's more casual connections. Viadeo offers business professionals the opportunity to communicate with others in their profession, to hunt for new jobs, and promote themselves to recruiters and potential employers, as well as enhance their reputations by making themselves more visible. Viadeo offers status updates, blogs, activity streams, events, group communication tools, company-specific pages, mobile apps, and plenty other services. Like LinkedIn, Viadeo has free and premium membership accounts and various marketing products and services sold to professional job recruiters. Retrieved from http://www.viadeo.com/en/connexion/

55 Wikispaces is run by Tangient, LLC—www.tangient.com. Since early 2005 the creators of Wikispaces have been dedicated to building the world's easiest to use wiki service by listening closely to the ever growing Wikispaces community. Retrieved from http://www.wikispaces.com/

56 RSS (most commonly expanded as really simple syndication) is a family of web feed formats used to publish frequently updated works—such as blog entries, news headlines, audio, and video—in a standardized format. RSS feed readers offer one of the most efficient ways to follow news, website and software updates newsletters, blogs and more. Many of the best news aggregators for Windows are available for free. The top free Windows RSS feed readers/news aggregators include: Omea Reader—http://www.omea-reader.en.softonic.com/; Awasu Personal Edition—http://www.awasu.com/; Google Reader—http://www.google.com/reader/view/; RSS Bandit—http://www.rssbandit.org/; SharpReader—http://www.sharpreader.net/; Mozilla Thunderbird—http://www.mozilla.org/en-US/thunderbird/; and BlogEx-

ing regularly changing web content; in other words, a family of web feed formats used to publish frequently updated works—such as blog entries, news headlines, audio, and video—in a standardized format, a tool most NGOs and INGOs are using today. With this tool many news-related sites, weblogs and other online publishers syndicate their content as an RSS Feed to whoever wants it.

- Yahoo! Messenger[57] is an all-in-one communication tool, and anyone, anywhere in the world, with a computer and Internet connection can use it.
- YouTube[58] is a video-sharing website on which users can upload, view and share videos.

The social media tools—Facebook, Yahoo Messenger, Twitter and YouTube—have been critical in organizing protests and have played important roles in Iran's 2009 presidential elections, also nicknamed the "Twitter Revolution" (The Washington Times, 2009). The Islamic Republic of Iran has always been a hub of cyber activity. Iran is one of the top 10 world's active blogging communities, with an estimated 700,000 bloggers. The Internet is celebrated as an agent of social change because of the level of censorship inside the country. The Internet is changing things in Iran, in ways which neither the government nor the

press—http://www.blogexpress.en.softonic.com/

57   Yahoo! Messenger (sometimes abbreviated YIM or YM) is an advertisement-supported instant messaging client and associated protocol provided by Yahoo! Yahoo! Messenger is provided free of charge and can be downloaded and used with a generic "Yahoo! ID" which also allows access to other Yahoo! Services, such as Yahoo! Mail, where users can be automatically notified when they receive new email. Retrieved from http://www.messenger.yahoo.com/

58   YouTube is the world's most popular online video community that allows billions of people to discover, watch, and share originally-created videos. YouTube provides a forum for people to connect, inform, and inspire others across the globe and acts as a distribution platform for original content creators and advertisers large and small. Retrieved from http://www.youtube.com/

democracy movement could have anticipated (Srebeny & Khiabany, 2010).

Also, social applications are empowering farmers in Africa who are using mobile phones to do business (Gakuru & Stepman, 2009). Nonprofits like the Grameen Foundation[59] and Kiwanja.net[60] are pumping grant money into projects to bring 'short message service' (SMS) applications to the developing world. There seems to be a market for mobile services in places like Southeast Asia and rural Africa, with a projected number of mobile phone subscribers expected to reach 4.5 billion globally by 2012 (roughly two-thirds of those in developing countries). There is no shortage of subscribers, even in poverty-stricken parts of the world. The Grameen Foundation in collaboration with Google is launching SMS applications in Africa with the ability to market goods via text message—almost like Craigslist[61] or eBay[62]. Kiwanja.net's Mobility Project is creating a new class of mobile applica-

---

59   Grameen Foundation, a nonprofit organization headquartered in Washington, DC, with an office in Seattle, Washington, was founded in 1997 by friends of Grameen Bank to help microfinance practitioners and spread the Grameen philosophy worldwide. The Foundation shares the ideas of 2006 Nobel Peace Laureate Muhammad Yunus. Grameen Foundation and Grameen Bank are independent organizations and have no financial or institutional links. Retrieved from http://www.grameenfoundation.org/

60   Since 2003, kiwanja.net has been helping empower local, national and international non-profit organizations to make better use of information and communications technology in their work. Specializing in the application of mobile technology, it provides a wide range of ICT-related services drawing on over 25 years' experience of its founder, Ken Banks. Nonprofits in over fifty countries have so far benefited from a range of kiwanja initiatives, including FrontlineSMS and nGOmobile. Retrieved from http://kiwanja.net/

61   Craigslist is a registered mark in the U.S. Patent and Trademark Office, providing local classifieds and forums; community moderated, and largely free. Retrieved from http://www.craigslist.org/about/sites

62   With more than 88 million active users globally, eBay is the world's largest online marketplace, where practically anyone can buy and sell practically anything. Founded in 1995, eBay connects a diverse and passionate community of individual buyers and sellers, as well as small businesses. Retrieved from http://www.ebayinc.com/

tion developers in Africa with a new set of development tools. Mobile service providers like South Africa's MTN are already moving into this market.

The use of OCL for advocacy by NGOs

NGOs are the front line troops tackling civil society and development issues. Although there are many different definitions debated in the research literature, development NGOs are "self-governing, private, not-for-profit organizations that are geared to improving the quality of life for disadvantaged people" (Vakil, 1997, p. 2060). During the past decade or so, there has been a rapid growth in the numbers and profile of development NGOs. This has been the case both in the industrialized countries of the North, where NGOs are concerned with poverty reduction and social justice work at home and abroad, and in aid-recipient resource-scarce countries of the South, where NGOs have been identified as potential partners both by governments and international aid agencies (Salamon, 1994; Smillie, 1995). NGOs are a diverse family of organizations, ranging from small local groups operating on a largely voluntary and informal basis to large-scale formal development agencies with multi-million dollar budgets and thousands of professional paid staff.

Funding institutions have two main options to support the social sector. The first is to create and fund a program from scratch. The second and often better option is funding a local NGO that has the credibility, network of contacts, understanding and trust already developed in the community it serves. What NGO's need most in the Internet space is an understanding of how they can more effectively facilitate their missions, technical and financial help in defining their net presence and assistance employing online tools effectively. Advocacy NGOs are well advised to acquire the hardware, the software, and the familiarity with the techniques so that they can effectively utilize information that is relevant to their activities and delivery mechanism.

There are significant advantages with the use of OCL for advocacy by NGOs. OCL technologies, and, in particular, the Internet, provide the public and individuals with access to information and sources and enable all to participate actively in the communication process. Internet connectivity is of special significance to civil society. Computer networks greatly facilitate participation at all levels—within groups, between groups, and between groups and their constituencies—thus helping to strengthen the organizations of civil society. Many NGOs, including human rights organizations, have embraced the ability to use the Internet to collect, cross-correlate and share information relatively easily and cheaply. The nonprofit organization Global Voices[63] is successful as an international community of bloggers who report on blogs and citizen media from around the world. What Global Voices does as an advocacy NGO is calling to attention to the most interesting conversations and perspectives emerging from citizens' media around the world by linking to text, photos, podcasts, video and other forms of grassroots citizens' media. The organization also facilitates the emergence of new citizens' voices through training, online tutorials, and publicizing the ways in which open-source and free tools can be used safely by people around the world to express themselves. And it advocates for freedom of expression around the world and protect the rights of journalists to report n events and opinions without fear of censorship or persecution.

The fundamental premise of NGO advocacy is about organized efforts to effect systematic change. NGOs are value based organizations of citizens with a motivation and desire for a better world for the poor and disadvantaged. The why and how of globally connected learning manifests by global competencies, connections, collaboration and communication to tools and projects designed and created for NGO development work to impact communities, bring in perspective, knowledge, skill and

---

63   Global Voices seeks to aggregate, curate, and amplify the global conversation online—shining light on places and people other media often ignore. Global Voices work to develop tools, institutions and relationships that will help all voices, everywhere, to be heard. Retrieved from http://globalvoicesonline.org/

disposition. As research continues to suggest that use of OCL tools can have excellent outcomes for NGOs, many NGO managers are finding in ways to blend the best of both worlds, combining time-tested practices of development work practices with powerful OCL tools to produce rich, engaging development work experiences. The Internet has seen impressive growth in user-driven applications such as blogs, podcasts and social networking sites. Online applications increasingly support the creation of value by social networks of people. When surveying the literature on online collaborative competencies, it becomes apparent that the phenomenon continues to grow in popularity and penetration across the globe. Users all over the world blog, network, tag and review. Social and development networking sites have entered the mainstream and now attract users across all generations and levels of society. The elements of advocacy as used by NGOs involve:

- advocacy effort that involves citizens in the advocacy process—an involvement that is conscious, intentional and democratic; and
- advocacy effort directed toward specific and identified disadvantaged groups.

NGO advocacy is therefore a systematic, democratic and organized effort by NGOs to change, influence or initiate policies, laws, practices and behavior so that disadvantaged citizens will be benefitted. OCL technologies' role in NGO advocacy is more of an educator through information dissemination, or the role of an opinion maker through persuasion. The value of digital technologies is being recognized by NGOs and governments as increasingly important in advocacy terms and as a means of supporting local and global development agendas. Of specific relevance of OCL is emphasis on development knowledge and practice sharing, which is regarded as being of particular importance to development work. The overall objective to ensure that development framework, so essential to the growth of the sector, continues to keep abreast of technological changes affecting how development knowledge is created and disseminated. To achieve this objective, the most significant issues are:

- improving awareness about development knowledge management; and
- promoting mechanisms to support the wholesale use of OCL technologies to strengthen NGO advocacy activities.

Internet as driving force of NGO advocacy: Knowledge is power and the Internet provides increased channels for understanding the world more rapidly while sharing experiences and information. As far as the character of NGO advocacy goes, the possibilities of the Internet must not be overlooked as the contributing factor. Whether it is globalvoicesonline. org, oneworldtrust.org or groups of private concerned netizens, all of them progressively and rapidly promoted the formation of an Internet culture for the public good. And this culture provided NGOs with a growing number of fresh troops. As far as existing NGOs are concerned, the Internet has therefore strengthened their capacity to a certain extent.

- **The Internet provides the capacity to support NGO advocacy by breaking through publishing restrictions.** Many NGOs today can now have their own online publications. The content and page format of these electronic publications may not compare with those of formal publications, but writers can freely expand on cutting-edge issues and share their personal experiences and views online. Through the medium of electronic publication, advocacy NGOs now have the opportunity to more efficiently communicate and exchange ideas with one another.

- **The Internet accelerates access to government information.** One important NGO task is advocating for government reform and enactment of laws and policies that guarantee human rights. The foundation of this advocacy built upon both production of cutting-edge investigative reports, as well as an understanding of government information and figures concerning laws, regulations, policies, programs, action plans, financial investments, and statistical reports. Although the richness of content varies among websites of different levels of government, there is already a great deal of information available on these websites. The Internet promotes international exchange. So theoretically, advocacy NGOs could understand development work, practice and establish contact with various constituents. For example, the Aid Workers Network[64] website offers a great deal of nonprofit data and enables aid workers to share practical advice and resources with each other. The Global Directory of Funding Agencies[65] website offers a great deal of nonprofit data and is an online platform designed with a vision of making resource available for organizations working in development. The United Nations is both a participant and a witness to an increasingly global civil society. More and more, nongovernmental organizations and other civil society organizations are UN system partners and valuable UN links to civil society. CSOs play a key role at major United Nations Conferences and are indispensable partners for UN efforts at the country levels.

- **The Internet has made it easy to highlight and address grassroots issues.** Stories highlighting social problems

---

64   Aid Workers Network is a free service where aid workers around the world can find practical help in the Advice Pages, check Blogs from aid workers, read interesting articles and swap tips in Aid Workers Exchange, learn about developing a career in aid and raising funds, and earn about the Aid Workers Network history and management. Retrieved from http://www.aidworkers.net/

65   FundingDirectory.info is an online directory of funding agencies with all profiles of leading development agencies supporting the development interventions in various part of the globe. The directory offers other related products and services related for effective resources mobilizations for the development agency with the like-minded organization in the sector. Retrieved from http://www.fundingdirectory.info/

can today be posted on the Internet—or issue a petition on an issue—over the Internet and wait for public opinion to foment. For example, an advocacy NGO can reach many other NGOs and volunteers through email groups and other methods.

- **The Internet helps strengthen connections among civil society organizations.** In addition to using popular instant messaging tools such as QQ[66], MSN and Skype, NGOs have established QQ groups, email ground, online forums, and information exchange sites to share information. This enables NGOs to realize one of the most basic Internet functions—building virtual communities and convening meetings that cross space and time.

Civil society actors energized by the Internet still face heavy resistance: Although the Internet offers development opportunities for civil society in the ways described above, there are still challenges faced by NGOs' use of the Internet. Most NGOs in developing countries exist in inferior environments and most lack a regular source of funding. Besides, the pace of progress in science and technology is fast and NGOs are finding it hard to cope and do not understand the technology landscape.

Also, there are common widespread attacks on users of webmail like Google[67], Yahoo! and Hotmail using sophisticated attack code. This code, which targets the web browser Internet Explorer 10[68], can be used by anyone, and a fix is yet to be built. The code specifically targets Gmail

---

66   QQ is real-time messaging that lets users share instant peer-to-peer file transfers (like MP3's) and chat in line integrated and moderated chatrooms. Retrieved from http://www.qq.co.za/

67   Google enables users to search the Web. Google features include PageRank, caching and translation of results, and an option to find similar pages. Retrieved from http://www.google.com/

68   Internet Explorer 10 (IE10) is the version of the Internet Explorer web browser released by Microsoft in 2012, and is the default browser in Windows 8. Retrieved from http://www.internet-explorer-10-preview. en.softonic.com/

accounts of journalists and human-rights advocacy groups. There has been a consistent pattern of infiltration and surveillance of email used by NGOs and journalists worldwide. "Phishing" or spoofed email is an increasing problem for email users. These types of messages look like they come from a legitimate source asking for account information. These email scams are becoming more sophisticated and widespread. The phishing email directs consumers to spoof websites that look like the real thing. The goal is always the same—to get financial information. And webmail providers and governments both want to keep this very quiet. The best possible solutions to anticipate any such attacks are low tech approaches. For the most highly sensitive work, it is recommended to always create a ghost, i.e. a separate, highly obscure online identity. It is also reasonable to use a new throwaway webmail address for each project; avoid using names in emails; develop slang terms for searchable phrases; and never link accounts together (and avoid connections between a known identity and the ghost email or a known identity connected to a Facebook profile, etc.). The Electronic Frontier Foundation (EFF)[69] has made recommendations on some long term solutions to provide Internet users with better options for secure communication.

- Internet users dealing with highly sensitive information are advised not to use Internet Explorer and should rather switch to a current version of the Firefox browser, which can be downloaded free from http://www.getfirefox.com.

- A very simple fix that also prevents much infiltration of online services is frequent updates of passwords at least

---

69   The Electronic Frontier Foundation (EFF) has created this Surveillance Self-Defense site to educate the American public about the law and technology of government surveillance in the United States, providing the information and tools necessary to evaluate the threat of surveillance and take appropriate steps to defend against it. Surveillance Self-Defense (SSD) exists to answer two main questions: What can the government legally do to spy on your computer data and communications? And what can you legally do to protect yourself against such spying?
Retrieved from https://ssd.eff.org/

quarterly. It is advised that strong webmail passwords (long with letters and numbers) are used.

- Again it is recommended for users to often run current anti-virus and anti-malware software.

- Also, often, public Internet café computers are compromised by intelligence services. Any information plugged into a public Internet café computer machine (like email password) can be intercepted and misused. This is where ghost accounts and "security through obscurity" are very useful.

- Use a "Virtual Private Network"[70] service to avoid any snooping and be better prepared to beat censorship. Virtual Private Networking is a method by which a user can access an organization's internal network over the Internet in a secure manner. A VPN provides users who are not on that internal network, secure access to resources inside it. This is done by creating tunnels that wrap data packets destined for the internal network and then encrypting those packets to send them across the Internet. Such programming is currently being built into a program called Indaba Global[71] (a next genera-

---

70   A virtual private network (VPN) is a network that uses a public telecommunication infrastructure and their technology such as the Internet, to provide remote offices or individual users with secure access to their organization's network. It aims to avoid an expensive system of owned or leased lines that can be used by only one organization. The goal of a VPN is to provide the organization with the same secure capabilities but at a much lower cost. It encapsulates data transfers between two or more networked devices not on the same private network so as to keep the transferred data private from other devices on one or more intervening local or wide area networks. There are many different classifications, implementations, and uses for VPNs. Retrieved from http://en.wikipedia.org/wiki/Virtual_private_network

71   Indaba Global has developed a software platform that is customizable with complete flexibility of offering secure access to online video training, audio and testing. Whether a firm's needs are for a specific product to be marketed to a targeted group (either securely or non-securely), or in need

tion fieldwork platform). In the interim, users can use a free VPN called "Hotspot Shield"[72], which is supported by ads; and OpenVPN[73], a virtual network software that provides secure, reliable, and scalable communication services, not only fulfilling the requirements of the traditional virtual private network market, but also addressing the demands of next wave web-scale VPN services. And it is recommended a Firefox plug-in called AdBlockPlus[74], which blocks the ads, is used with this free VPN. HotSpot Shield also gives users a random IP address, which defeats most local censorship. HotSpot Shield can be downloaded from Anchor-Free[75] at http://www.anchorfree.com/ Hotspot Shield.

---

of production of an educational program, Indaba offers hands-on, proven expertise to provide prompt and impressive results. Indaba Global's flexible software and eLearning platform capabilities offers an affordable and results-oriented solution. Retrieved from www.indaba1.com/

72   Hotspot Shield creates a virtual private network (VPN) between your laptop or iPhone and our Internet gateway. This impenetrable tunnel prevents snoopers, hackers, ISP's, from viewing your web browsing activities, instant messages, downloads, credit card information or anything else you send over the network. Hotspot Shield security application is free to download, employs the latest VPN technology, and is easy to install and use. Retrieved from http://hotspotshield.com/

73   OpenVPN Technologies is a privately held company based in the Pleasanton, California, integrating a suite of leading-edge networking and software technologies. Retrieved from http://www.openvpn.net/

74   AdeblockPlus: Save your time and traffic - Annoyed by adverts? Troubled by tracking? Bothered by banners? Install Adblock Plus now to regain control of the internet and change the way that you view the web. You can also choose from over forty filter subscriptions to automatically configure the add-on for purposes ranging from removing online advertising to blocking all known malware domains. Retrieved from http://adblockplus.org/en/

75   Currently AnchorFree powers hundreds of millions of page views per month which are sold to advertisers looking for global reach and innovative engagement opportunities. Advertisers use AnchorFree to target online advertising video and display campaigns, targeted specifically to audience segments, channel verticals, contextual websites, and across all domains

And AdBlockPlus (a plug-in for Firefox browser) can be downloaded from https://addons.mozilla.org/en-US/firefox/addon/1865.

- Another prevention fix recommended is to lock up computer hard drives with disc encryption. It's very easy to lose a laptop, and afterwards it is common for the data on your PC to go onto a criminal market. It's also easy for an adversary to confiscate a PC and root through files. Fortunately, encryption software is free and works very well. A dependable encryption software recommended is using TrueCrypt[76], a full disc encryption. Encryption is fundamentally better from a Windows login password. TrueCrypt takes some time to set up, but is very stable and easy to use afterwards.

- Again, because every year 43% of computer users lose their music, photos, documents, and more, by default, the Carbonite[28] program has been developed to back up everything in 'Documents and Settings' folder (called 'Users' in Windows Vista), including documents, photos, email and data files from applications, such as Quicken, Money, etc. Once a subscription is purchased, music is also added to the list. The default backup does not include programs, system files, temporary files, vid-

---

visited by our users. AnchorFree's technology enables ad targeting across all domains, thus many advertisers utilize AnchorFree as a central hub for media buying across multiple domains and circumstances online. Retrieved from http://www.anchorfree.com/

76   The ultimate freeware encryption program, TrueCrypt is loaded with powerful features that those concerned with protecting their data from thievery should want--and have. It offers 11 algorithms for encrypting your private files in a password-protected volume. You can store your encrypted data in files (containers) or partitions (devices). TrueCrypt works hard to offer powerful data protection, recommending complex passwords, explaining the benefits of hidden volumes, and erasing telltale signs of the encryption process, including mouse movements and keystrokes. Retrieved from http://download.cnet.com/TrueCrypt/3000-2092_4-10527243.html?tag=mncol

eos, or individual files greater than 4GB. Users of the
program can, also, manually add these to Carbonite[77]
backup with the exception of system files located in C:\
Windows and temporary files located in Temp folders.

The use of OCL technologies as effective tools in the hands of organizations of civil society in order to advance both local and global agendas
has, nonetheless, proven itself in Latin America, China and South East
Asia and among global organizations of civil society such as human
rights groups and ecologically oriented organizations. This potential
empowerment of civil society organizations using OCL technologies
exists in Africa and the Middle Eastern regions as well. The Internet
has the ability to unleash the full potential of civil society in the developing regions of the world. ICTs are facilitating the decentralization of
power. The growing social economy, the research and development of
the Internet, satellite television, and growing knowledge economy are all
strengthening the democratic organizations of civil society. Information
system technologies tend to empower local communities, and under-
mining central influence tied to command-control authority structures.
The consequences arising from the use of information which was the
decisive trigger of the Islamic Revolution that brought about the change
from the Shah to the Ayatollah Khomeini in Iran in the 1970s is an
example where too much information of a modernizing nature may
have helped induce a reaction and a return to a fundamental Islamic
preference to exclude outside information. Yet, the irony is that, in his
quest for power, the Ayatollah carried out his revolution based on the
new use of communication technology. Cassette tapes were used to
foment the revolt that brought about the change—with tapes smuggled
into Iran by pilgrims returning from abroad then broadcast over loud-
speakers in mosques to supporters.

Contemporary social theorists have characterized these efforts to glo-
balize these social movements as 'globalization from below' claiming

---

77   Carbonite Online Backup protects computers from accidental deletion,
     theft, disaster and drive failure. It is a program that offers unlimited backup
     capacity. It is completely automatic, encrypted and secure with easy file
     recovery. Retrieved from http://carbonite.com/

that these movement structures operate by creating social connections with each other at grassroots level rather than by creating or maintaining existing power structures (Tomei, 2009). Moreover, NGOs function in politically complex systems, making it increasingly difficult for any one of them to manage effectively in isolation. Managing such complexity without enforceable rules of interaction is through some type of explicit and coherent community networking and inter-organizational collaboration (Walsh & Shaul, 1997). Given that partnership, NGOs often strive to cooperate in ways that usually take the shape of networking and information sharing to increase the impact of development programs. Safe to believe many NGOs globally are today currently dealing with a multitude of challenges and working either at or across the local, national or international level. These NGOs are using OCL technologies to contribute to the international and national discourse on issues of global scope, such as the eradication of poverty and the promotion of gender equality, peace, sustainable development and human rights. Most NGOs no longer work in isolation, but rather in networks that share information and other resources across borders. The increasing bulk of NGO networks and intensifying degree of NGO advocacy can be seen as a very influential organizational articulation of a global human rights enforcement mechanism and organizational advocacy for good governance in developing democracies (Salomon, et.al., 2001).

OCL technologies have therefore excelled as instruments for social change and persuasion. And in keeping with current emphasis on privatization of States economies, international aid has been increasingly channeled through NGOs and their expatriate technical experts to support social change programs in the developing world. Donor agencies have recognized the vibrant and thriving civil prominence of non-governmental organizations with their grass roots constituencies' efforts in poverty alleviation, social welfare and the development of civil society. NGOs are seen by these donor agencies as being more ecologically aware and resourceful providers than governments, especially in reaching the poor and marginalized communities.

Clearly, there is a significant relationship between advocacy groups' priorities and their action plans. More importantly, it is critical to understand the processes involved in translating collective priorities of NGOs into collective action—that is, which factors encourage social mobilization. These new technologies have also demonstrated the capacity to make one organization's advocacy strategies and actions visible to others. For developing countries, the digital revolution offers unprecedented opportunities and many have predicted the coming of an "Internet leadership" in these countries with governments that recognize the key role that technology in general and ICTs in particular play in national development. Even non-democratic regimes have not underestimated the power of ICTs because they too recognize the potential of ICTs to bolster or stabilize government operations. The Internet has overwhelming implications for any such governments which are dictatorships which often seek to restrict freedom of expression and related human rights. Civil society organizations remain steadfast domestically; advancing rights and demanding accountability and transparency, and they become a part of a global network of similar organizations. Internet options and possibilities have offered citizens enhanced access both to legal and factual, and have delivered contending interpretations of news and events within their country and worldwide. The Internet has also provided possibilities for individuals to find their voices even if they have to communicate surreptitiously. These features of the Internet have shown how common platforms help advance social change and are critically important for strengthening democracies, and putting up a formidable challenge against dictatorships.

The Internet is therefore clearly leading the way especially in influencing political systems. ICTs have the promise to be key to development, prosperity, and influence. Through email and web sites, human rights organizations with their variety of mandates and tasks have been able to disseminate information far more effectively than ever before, despite modest resources and limited access to local media technologies. In countries where local papers are censored, newspaper editors have been able to post banned online stories where local and international readers view them. For example, the censorship in China, which the government positively refers to as the Golden Shield Project (sometimes referred to as the Great Fire Wall) is part of what uses content filtering software "to protect its citizens from online dangers". With some creativity however, Netizens[78] have learned that it is possible to bypass the government's firewall and banned material can be accessed through VPNs without being blocked.

Also, the Internet has provided the Israeli and Arabs with tools—such as access to information and electronic discourse—to encourage mutual understanding and dialogue through the exchange of ideas. Websites and discussion systems such as Yossi Alpher's Bitterlemons.org[79] and Usenet[80] are impacting the way Arabs and Israelis and their supporters worldwide think about one another, suggesting that conflict can be replaced, or even best served, by dialogue rather than violence. The Internet's influences on democratic norms and modes, and participatory politics, particularly in Southern countries with little or no formal

---

78   Netizens use the Internet to engage in activities of extended social groups, such as giving and receiving viewpoints, furnishing information, fostering the Internet as an intellectual and a social resource, and making choices for the self-assembled communities. Generally, a netizen can be any user of the worldwide, unstructured forums of the Internet. Retrieved from http://en.wikipedia.org/wiki/Netizen

79   Bitterlemons.org is a website that presents Israeli and Palestinian viewpoints on prominent issues of concern. It focuses on the Palestinian-Israeli conflict and peace process. It is produced, edited and partially written by Ghassan Khatib, a Palestinian, and Yossi Alpher, an Israeli. Its goal is to contribute to mutual understanding through the open exchange of ideas. *Bitterlemons.org* aspires to impact the way Palestinians, Israelis and others worldwide think about the Palestinian-Israeli conflict. Retrieved from http://www.bitterlemons.org/about/about.html

80   Usenet is a world-wide distributed discussion system. It consists of a set of "newsgroups" with names that are classified hierarchically by subject. "Articles" or "messages" are "posted" to these newsgroups by people on computers with the appropriate software -- these articles are then broadcast to other interconnected computer systems via a wide variety of networks. Some newsgroups are "moderated"; in these newsgroups, the articles are first sent to a moderator for approval before appearing in the newsgroup. Usenet is available on a wide variety of computer systems and networks, but the bulk of modern Usenet traffic is transported over either the Internet or UUCP. Retrieved http://www.usenet.com/usenet.html

democratic institutions, is therefore rapidly gaining recognition on the part of NGOs, INGOs, and the academic research community.

The idea of a boundless information world, as it was conceptualized, is increasingly inculcated into cultures in a globalizing world. The goals are the same for all developing countries working to use these new technologies—to carve a new niche as well as empower their communities, find more efficient production systems and renew their national resource pools simultaneously. While some may point to the 'Digital Divide' regarding tele-density comparisons, the optimists have been contemplating on how to improve on knowledge capability in order to bridge the 'Digital Divide' (Norris, 2001). The 'Digital Bridge' (Afele, 2002) is what would enable developing Southern countries to successfully deploy information societies among its peoples; and such a knowledge bridge would actualize economic possibilities for the South—enabling communities to learn, solve problems, produce more efficiently and preserve and enrich national systems, fostering peace, among other advancements.

Chapter 4: OCL advances, social anxieties

To engage creatively with real world issues in the environment and underserved communities requires active leadership using distributed expertise from individuals, organizations and communities in diverse institutions and localized settings. Evidently, *critical global challenges* require a novel approach towards *sustainable design innovation*, one that embraces multidisciplinary expertise, open peer review and distributed contributions in the public domain. Recent trends with collaborative resource development models cover both "open source" software and open educational resources and suggest many benefits for facilitating creation, sharing, and reuse of design knowledge and allowing an "open" evolution of design based on public peer review and contributions from diverse participants for rapid design iteration.

Adciv.org[81], an online platform that provides an environment for *open collaborative design* in critical domains has been a resourceful platform for designers of NGO empowerment software. A core element of this development model is a principle called '*copyleft*' which is a way of applying copyright to a creative work in a way that makes sure that anyone can freely use it or build upon it—and also that derivative works inherit the same terms, ensuring anything based on the original is freely available. Global Advances Group[82] also offers solutions for social enterprises and non-profits. It is an IT and website assistance platform, giving non-profit and social organizations a voice through the Internet.

---

81 Adciv.org open collaborative design involves applying principles from the remarkable free and open-source software movement that provides a powerful new way to design physical objects, machines and systems. Open collaborative design is a nascent field that has huge potential to radically alter the way goods, machines and systems are created—not only for personal items but all the way up to components on national or global infrastructure. Retrieved from http://www.adciv.org/open_collaborative_design

82 Global Advances Group utilizes technology and the Internet to strengthen identities effectiveness and technical know-how of social ventures and non-profit organizations. Retrieved from http://www.globaladvances.com/social-and-non-profit

The fundamental tenet of any agile software development methodology is its ability to integrate online and computer based software for one-to-one and broadcast messages as a vital link among people. In software application development, agile software development (ASD) is a methodology for the creative process that anticipates the need for flexibility and applies a level of pragmatism into the delivery of the finished product. Agile software development focuses on keeping code simple, testing often, and delivering functional bits of the application as soon as they are ready. The building of a distributed software platform does not by itself create a culture of design innovation in such problem domains. However, the significance of a multidisciplinary approach to learning and cooperative design has since being recognized. Better understanding of the role of online tools, social incentives and barriers in the success of emerging design projects should provide a framework that informs future collaborative systems and pedagogical approaches towards sustainable design initiatives. People determine the kind of society they want. The design and deployment of new technologies is now done in ways that are most likely to further their goals. In this regard, institutional innovations are as important as scientific or technological breakthroughs in creating new opportunities for human development.

The major global anti-corruption "watchdog" organizations, Transparency International and Global Integrity, as well, use various OCL technologies to determine and assess corruption indices in all regions of the world. Transparency International has developed an Anti-Corruption Training Manual[83] specifically for the infrastructure, construction and engineering sectors to help users achieve a better understanding of corruption and how to avoid it. It is an online tool which can be used by individuals and by companies as part of their corporate training. Global Integrity uses an online tool to prepare its annual Global

---

83   The Anti-Corruption Training Manual aims to help users achieve a better understanding of corruption and how to avoid it. It can be used by individuals, and also by companies as part of their corporate training. Published by Transparency International and can be retrieved from http://www.ciob.org.uk/document/anti-corruption-training-manual

Integrity Reports, called MAGIC (Multi-user Access to Global Integrity Content[84])—a tool that is extensively used by its pool of researchers and peer reviewers to generate, synthesize, and disseminate credible, comprehensive and timely information on governance and corruption trends around the world.

Along with other social software tools and protocols such as weblogs, wikis and RSS feeds, which are particularly important aspects of contemporary technological innovation, is the quest for new ways to capture, store, process, transport and display information. Progress in this field will have a philosophical impression on societies and their agents for social change, though it is a challenge to foresee all of the future social and economic implications of the adoption and proliferation of new information and communication technologies.

Likewise, there has been considerable interest as well in e-Governance programs. E-Government involves changing entire systems in governments—targets, methods, processes, practices—and modernizing the functioning of government agencies. Information technology is the most important tool for effecting this change. E-Governance would mean changing public administration from personal and paper-based working to an on-line environment to provide efficient, better, and clear services, including increasing efficiency of public service delivery and revenue generation—by promoting human resource development in the field of ICTs. The objective of promoting e-Governance practices is to build the capacity of e-ready departments using software package consisting of open source-based programs on tax systems and business permits and licensing systems (Governance World Watch, 2007).

---

84   Indaba is a proposed software tool that **enables grassroots research teams to design, execute, peer review, aggregate, publish and export empirical research** of previously unquantifiable social performance factors. Indaba's primary leap forward from MAGIC (Multiuser Access to Global Integrity Content) is its ability to empower users with complete customization within a framework of best practices. Indaba goes well beyond enabling Global Integrity to measure good governance and anti-corruption; Indaba allows *anyone* measuring *any* fuzzy social issue to define the problem and track progress towards a solution.

ICTs are central to the new knowledge economy and are essential for the promotion of development especially with knowledge generated from the latest cutting-edge technologies. ICTs and their OCL capabilities present the developing countries with colossal opportunities and challenges, not only to expedite their development but also in helping to bridge the economic and prosperity gaps between them and the developed countries. They also present the developing countries with a unique opportunity to 'leap-frog' alternatives and economically feasible stages of development—for example, by going straight to mobile phones, cutting out landlines.

ICTs have opened up a new range of opportunities and some developing countries are making significant strides in trying to meet some of their aspirations for a better, knowledge-oriented culture and to catch up on the new experiences and opportunities to remain connected. The technological advancement developing countries are gravitating to is mirrored in development cooperation. International development institutions are now seeking more efficient ways to approach development effort—embracing different roles, acting as partners instead of donors; building local expertise instead of providing technical assistance; focusing on qualitative rather than quantitative results; and more generally reforming the way they work and who they work with. These trends inspire a need for system-level tools conducive to an environment that supports the creation and sharing of new ideas and knowledge. These tools need to be universal, user-friendly, and formidable instruments for socio-economic empowerment, capable of nurturing social change and democratization, accommodating of decentralization, and useful in that they provide social or significant benefits to those using them. For many people, new information and communications technologies are the right tools at the right time. If prudently utilized, investments in information, knowledge, and ICTs can help create jobs that produce wealth, build bridges between governments and citizens, forge relations among organizations and communities, and improve the delivery of fundamental services to under-served communities.

While the skeptics still contemplate about ICTs direct contribution to poverty alleviation, there are signs that ICTs can contribute to development goals if used properly based on local needs and circumstances. ICTs can contribute to even more development goals to include:

- enrichment of ideas;
- informal discourse and knowledge exchange that provide deeper understanding of the shared content;
- development of communication skills;
- socializing of the members within group interactions and community development activities;
- improved emotional and participatory support of the learning communities' members;
- high motivational level of participation and awareness of individual responsibility for the success in advocacy;
- development of the group advocacy experiences, which are more than the sum of individual experiences because of the interactive nature of the knowledge construction process; and
- learning through practice, learning as experience, making meaning in a social context;
- generate rural employment through trade facilitation; and
- greatly enhance the integration of the rural with the national economy, improve living standards, ameliorate feelings of isolation, and potentially stem the steady migration of people from the countryside to the cities.

The growing challenges of the underprivileged in developing societies of the South create a critical condition today for radical and innovative approaches towards *sustainable design*. Developmental economists like Amartya Sen and Jean Dreze (1999) have pointed out that the central feature in the process of development should be the *"expansion of human capabilities and freedoms"*. Sen and Dreze (1999) have observed that gains from economic growth are seldom used into fixing the problems of marginalized communities or necessarily creating jobs or social opportunities for all. Expanding human capabilities and freedoms, therefore, requires a conscious design approach that provides greater access to affordable clean water, sanitation, and healthcare; education and employment; and rights to political participation. The unique experiences and expertise of individuals in diverse institutions and localized settings can be of real value to the process. Innovation may become apparent by a combination of individual and cooperative efforts, while sharing and access requires yet another range of mechanisms and channels. And there has to be copious knowledge networks and dialogue among stakeholders, domain experts, entrepreneurs and field-organizations to make any design processes participatory; and the emerging concepts open to peer-review, and the outcomes sustainable and accessible to all. What is needed in the new 'knowledge society' is diversity; a multitude of knowledge brokers, a Babel of banks. Where ICTs can make a real difference is in providing access to these different and competitive data banks (which is all the so-called 'knowledge banks' can claim to be), which in turn enables all humanity, through the media and civil society fora, to engage in well-informed, constructive and democratic debate.

Moreover, Sub-Saharan Africa, especially, must step up its engagement with ICT in order to meet up the challenges of the 21st Century. Knowing the importance of these technologies in shaping wellbeing is reason enough to justify why ICT must be given a stronger role in bringing a better perspective to development issues in Sub-Saharan Africa.

- Firstly the use of websites, tele-centers and community radios can better the participation of women and poor people in development debates.

- More so, awareness to the prevalence of diseases and healthcare services therefore will be facilitated while rural and urban barriers can be shrunk through internet links. Worth noting that movement of traditional mails to and from these areas is marred by poor road networks and poor postal infrastructural systems.

- ICTs also facilitate the building of synergies and partnerships between development stakeholders and organizations. A good example is the Eldis Community which can boast of bringing together over 4000 development professionals and organizations.

- Besides, ICTs can be used as weapons to moderate autocratic systems. Modern trends towards this direction were witnessed in the post Iranian election crises.

- Moreover, ICTs facilitate the identification and isolation of development workers, organizations, donors and charities. This is positive as these resources can be used in the design and implementation of interventions aimed at poverty reduction more easily than it was during pre-ICTs era.

- ICTs will also facilitate data collection and publishing of research and fieldwork of NGOs, Civil Society Organizations etc. ICTs can surely be used for the public good.

- Farmer Field Schools, Climate Change Schools and other teaching initiatives will have better content if researched materials and tested practices can easily be accessed during particular programs. A good example of an initiative that can be upgraded with more ICTs is the UNESCO teaching initiative, Concept Note[85]. Other areas where ICTs will play a key role in improving well-being in Sub-Saharan Africa include processes about isolating pastoral and common resources in Africa (IFAD, 2010), women and microfinance, improving human rights and involving excluded groups and gen-

---

85   The purpose of this Concept Note is to provide an overview of UNESCO's Teacher Training Initiative for Sub-Saharan Africa (TTISSA). The Concept Note serves to help build a shared understanding of what TTISSA is, the principles underpinning the initiative, the way in which it will be developed and implemented and the way in which there will be engagement with other stakeholders to draw on expertise and enhance the impact of TTISSA as well as that of other related initiatives. Retrieved from http://unesdoc.unesco.org/images/0015/001539/153939E.pdf

der mainstreaming which are all vital to stable modern, just and prosperous societies.

- With ICTs the poor, women and other marginal segments will cease to be considered as passive victims but as pro-active participants in development as livelihoods strategies will be better understood and collected for a better development management.

- And the re-imaging of Africa as place with business potential, active citizens and progressive cultures can more easily be achieved via ICTs. Social networking sites like Facebook, YouTube, NGO Connect[86], etc. have also recently helped in the shaping of positive perspectives about Africa as they report and share African development initiatives virtually and worldwide.

There are already many initiatives worthy of note seeking to improve access to ICTs in Africa. These interventions strive at improving governance and wellbeing via informed data on African sub-populations with the use of contemporary information and communication technologies. Some important interventions in Africa include the following:

- The Catalyzing Access to ICT in Africa (CATIA)[87] program which explores ways of improving access to ICTs

---

86   NGOConnect.NET, offers a dynamic site dedicated to connecting and strengthening non-governmental organizations (NGOs), networks and support organizations worldwide. Here you will find many of the best tools, theoretical frameworks; innovations and lessons learned that the NGO community, donors and support organizations worldwide have to offer. Retrieved from http://www.ngoconnect.net/home

87   The Catalyzing Access to ICT in Africa (CATIA) program aims to enable poor people in Africa to gain maximum benefit from the opportunities offered by Information and Communication Technology (ICT) and to act as a strong catalyst for reform. It will support a package of strategic activities to improve affordable access to the full range of ICTs, from Internet to community radio. This program is focused on the need for ICTs to address social and economic development issues. It will be working to help build capacity across Africa to achieve sustainable change. Retrieved from http://www.catia.ws

by poor sub-populations as a catalyzing tool towards social reforms and development.

- LINK Centre (University of the Witwatersrand) working as a leading stakeholder in regulation, management, training and research on ICTs in Southern Africa.
- Acacia which is an international initiative buttressing ways to empower communities to use ICTs to relevant issues about their immediate livelihoods realities.
- APC (Africa ICT Policy Monitor)[88] is an intervention of the Association for Progressive Communications (APC) which aims to help African civil society organizations use information and communication technologies (ICT) policy development to achieve an Information Society based on social justice, democracy and human rights.
- Research ICT Africa[89] focuses on policy and regulation research in African ICTs.
- The Englewood, Colorado-based Liberty Global's venture capital arm is investing in bringing affordable Inter-

---

88   The primary goal of the APC Africa ICT Policy Monitor is to enable African civil society organizations to engage in ICT policy development processes in order to promote an information society based on social justice and human rights. The ultimate aim is for governments and policy-makers to recognize that access to and the use of ICTs is a basic human right. The project, which was started in 2001, focuses on nine African countries where APC is working: South Africa, Zimbabwe, Kenya, Uganda, Democratic Republic of Congo, Nigeria, Senegal, Ethiopia, and Egypt. It covers several thematic areas, including access, communication rights, internet governance, and telecommunications. The policy monitor also publishes the Chakula e-newsletter. Chakula, a Swahili word for 'food', highlights ICT policy advocacy issues in line with APC's work on the ground. Retrieved from http://www.apc.org/en/home

89   The Research ICT Africa Network conducts research on ICT policy and regulation that facilitates evidence-based and informed policy making for improved access, use and application of ICT for social development and economic growth. Retrieved from http://www.researchictafrica.net/

net access to Africa and other parts of the developing world now bypassed by the Internet. LGI Ventures[90] is helping bankroll a Jersey, England-based satellite venture, 03B[91], that landed $1 billion in debt and equity funding, with money from satellite giants SES[92], Google,

---

90   Liberty Global, Inc. ("Liberty Global") is the leading international cable operator offering advanced video, telephone, and broadband internet services. We operate broadband communications networks in 14 countries principally located in Europe operating under the brands UPC, Unitymedia (Germany), Cablecom (Switzerland) and Telenet (Belgium), VTR (Chile), and AUSTAR (Australia). Liberty Global's operations also include significant media and programming businesses such as Chellomedia, a world class multimedia content provider based in Europe, as well as interests in content businesses in each of our regional markets. Through the efforts of 20,0001 employees worldwide, Liberty Global connects 17.7 million customers to the world of information, communications, and entertainment. As of September 30, 2010, Liberty Global's networks passed approximately 31.2 million homes and served more than 27.5 million Revenue Generating Units (RGUs), including approximately 16.8 million video subscribers, of which 7.7 million were digital cable and Direct-to-Home (DTH) satellite subscribers, 6.2 million broadband internet subscribers, and 4.5 million voice subscribers. Retrieved from http://www.lgi.com/

91   O3b is building a next-generation network that combines the reach of satellite with the speed of fiber. O3b's groundbreaking services will enable emerging market telcos and ISPs to make the internet a truly global and universal experience. With world-class financial and operational support from SES, HSBC, LibertyGlobal, Development Bank of South Africa, Sofina, Satya Capital, Google, Northbridge Venture Partners, Allen & Company, O3b is creating a global internet backbone to serve several billion consumers, businesses and other organizations in more than 150 countries. Retrieved from http://www.o3bnetworks.com/

92   SES is a world-leading telecommunications satellite operator, with a global fleet of more than 40 geostationary satellites that can reach 99% of the world's population. SES satellites are the world's leading television distribution platform, broadcasting the equivalent of more than 100,000 hours of television programming every day, and providing vital communications services and broadband access to businesses and to government administrations worldwide. SES operates mainly through SES ASTRA and SES WORLD SKIES and holds participations in satellite operators QuetzSat, Ciel, O3b Networks, YahLive and in a number of satellite service provision

and financial services company HSBC[93] Holdings—for offering wholesale Internet access by satellite.

The work of Microsoft, through its "unlimited potential vision", in this regard, with a commitment to making technology more affordable, relevant and accessible for the 5 billion people around the world who do not yet enjoy its benefits is a laudable effort in the right direction. Microsoft is partnering with UNESCO and hopes to transform education and inspire a culture of collaborative innovation and research and development, and through these means enable better jobs and opportunities. "By working with governments, intergovernmental organizations, nongovernmental organizations and industry partners in under-served communities in developing regions of the world, Microsoft hopes to reach its first major milestone—to reach the next 1 billion people who are not yet realizing the benefits of technology—by 2015" (Microsoft, 2008).

However, multilaterals, doing operational development work in the digital divide area, must listen more to local constituencies and develop projects based on real local need versus perceived need as defined by inter-agency officials. They must be flexible and fund local initiatives. A few multilaterals and government aid agencies do distinguish themselves in this area. The UNDP has allowed OSI[94] access to the unique

---

companies. Retrieved from http://www.ses.com/ses/welcome/

93   Headquartered in London, HSBC is one of the largest banking and financial services organizations in the world. HSBC's international network comprises around 8,000 offices in 87 countries and territories in Europe, the Asia-Pacific region, the Americas, the Middle East and Africa. With listings on the London, Hong Kong, New York, Paris and Bermuda stock exchanges, shares in HSBC Holdings plc are held by around 220,000 shareholders in 124 countries and territories. The shares are traded on the New York Stock Exchange in the form of American Depositary Receipts. HSBC provides a comprehensive range of financial services to around 100 million customers through four customer groups and global businesses: Personal Financial Services (including consumer finance); Commercial Banking; Global Banking and Markets; and Private Banking. Retrieved from http://www.hsbc.com/

94   The *Open System Interconnection (OSI)* protocol suite is comprised of numerous standard protocols that are based on the OSI reference model.

resources it brings to the table in workable project partnerships locally. It has effectively brought people together across sectors to work on Internet policy issues in some countries as well. It is one of the first multilaterals to have developed a relationship with a major corporate partner (CISCO[95]) to fund digital divide projects focusing on poverty alleviation. Notable in this latter example is that to facilitate this partnership, a totally independent organization, Netaid[96], is being created outside the UNDP bureaucracy. NATO has done some infrastructural funding in Central and Eastern Europe, but it is more notable for the network training and management conferences it supports working with local and regional associations. The Canadian International Development Agency[97] (CIDA) and International Development Research

---

These protocols are part of an international program to develop data-networking protocols and other standards that facilitate multivendor equipment interoperability. The OSI program grew out of a need for international networking standards and is designed to facilitate communication between hardware and software systems despite differences in underlying architectures. The OSI specifications were conceived and implemented by two international standards organizations: the International Organization for Standardization (ISO) and the International Telecommunication Union-Telecommunications Standards Sector (ITU-T). Retrieved from http://www.cisco.com/en/US/docs/internetworking/technology/handbook/OSI-Protocols.html. OSI funded a project called Probono.net. It is an online resource for lawyers who wish to do free legal work. This is a specialized area of law and if lawyers have to root around to find resources in addition to doing work for free, they are less likely to volunteer. Retrieved from http://www.probono.net/

95   For more than two decades, Cisco's vision has been to change the way the world works, lives, plays, and learns. Our approach to corporate social responsibility (CSR) aligns responsible business practices and social investments to create long-term value for our business. Cisco is engaging the power of the human network to transform societies, create a thriving employee experience, govern our business, develop products responsibly, and protect the environment. Retrieved from http://www.cisco.com/

96   Net-Aid was founded in 1999, with the goal of providing technology for small businesses and non-profit organizations in an effective and cost efficient manner. Retrieved from http://www.net-aid.net/index.html

97   The Canadian International Development Agency (CIDA) is Canada's lead agency for development assistance. CIDA's aim is to: manage Canada's

Council[98] (IDRC) are standouts in doing technology and development work. Finally, support should be given to NGOs in the business of delivering successful technology solutions and working in the arena of the digital divide. The Internet Society[99] has done an excellent job of providing training to developing countries starting out on the Information highway. A number of important policy organizations and associations are also involved in insuring NGOs and individuals have a say in Internet governance as well as advocating for appropriate Internet policy throughout the world. The Center for Democracy and Technology[100] (CDT), Computer Professionals for Social Responsibility[101] (CPSR),

---

support and resources effectively and accountably to achieve meaningful, sustainable results and; engage in policy development in Canada and internationally, enabling Canada's effort to realize its development objectives. Retrieved from http://www.acdi-cida.gc.ca/home

98 The International Development Research Council is a student-created, student-led group at the University of Notre Dame. IDRC seeks to help students educate themselves and each other about the ever-changing field of international development and, thus, prepare to enter the world as true leaders. Retrieved from http://www.nd.edu/~idrc/IDRC/Welcome.html

99 The Internet Society (ISOC) is a nonprofit organization founded in 1992 to provide leadership in Internet related standards, education, and policy. With offices in Washington D.C., USA, and Geneva, Switzerland, it is dedicated to ensuring the open development, evolution and use of the Internet for the benefit of people throughout the world. The Internet Society provides leadership in addressing issues that confront the future of the Internet, and is the organizational home for the groups responsible for Internet infrastructure standards, including the Internet Engineering Task Force (IETF) and the Internet Architecture Board (IAB). Retrieved from http://www.isoc.org/

100 The Center for Democracy and Technology is a non-profit public interest organization working to keep the Internet open, innovative, and free. As a civil liberties group with expertise in law, technology, and policy, CDT works to enhance free expression and privacy in communications technologies by finding practical and innovative solutions to public policy challenges while protecting civil liberties. CDT is dedicated to building consensus among all parties interested in the future of the Internet and other new communications media. Retrieved from http://www.cdt.org/

101 CPSR is a global organization promoting the responsible use of com-

The Electronic Privacy Information Center[102] (EPIC), Global Internet Liberty Campaign[103] (GILC), Electronic Frontier Foundation (EFF) are just a few of the entities that occupy this important space.

---

puter technology. Founded in 1981, CPSR educates policymakers and the public on a wide range of issues. CPSR has incubated numerous projects such as Privaterra, the Public Sphere Project, EPIC (the Electronic Privacy Information Center), the 21st Century Project, the Civil Society Project, and the CFP (Computers, Freedom & Privacy) Conference. Originally founded by U.S. computer scientists, CPSR now has members in 26 countries on six continents. Retrieved from http://cpsr.org/

102   EPIC is a public interest research center in Washington, D.C. It was established in 1994 to focus public attention on emerging civil liberties issues and to protect privacy, the First Amendment, and constitutional values. EPIC publishes an award-winning e-mail and online newsletter on civil liberties in the information age - the EPIC Alert. We also publish reports and even books about privacy, open government, free speech, and other important topics related to civil liberties. Retrieved from http://epic.org/

103   The Global Internet Liberty Campaign was formed at the annual meeting of the Internet Society in Montreal. Members of the coalition include the American Civil Liberties Union, the Electronic Privacy Information Center, Human Rights Watch, the Internet Society, Privacy International, the Association des Utilisateurs d'Internet, and other civil liberties and human rights organizations. Retrieved from http://gilc.org/index.html

It shouldn't be too much of a surprise that the Internet has evolved into a force strong enough to reflect the greatest hopes and fears of those who use it. After all, it was designed to withstand nuclear war, not just the puny huffs and puffs of politicians and religious fanatics.

Denise Caruso, digital commerce columnist,
– New York Times

Part II:

Accountability and Online Collaborative Learning as means to social change

Introduction

Accountability in the operations of all local and international NGOs (mainly humanitarian, development and human rights organizations) is essential. NGOs do have a particular responsibility to lead by example and shine as beacons of legitimacy and accountability. They are often entrusted with funds from third parties including individuals, trusts, foundations and corporate philanthropy, as well as tax-payer funds. Governments in many developed countries have embraced the principles of new public management. These principles empower NGOs in developed countries with public (tax-payer) funds to provide services to communities based on rigid rules of operations and reporting guidelines. The May 2003 American Enterprise Institute[104] co-sponsored conference with the Bush administration on the theme '*We're not from the Government, but we are here to help you: The growing power of an unelected few*' is testament to the relevance given to NGOs by the government in the United States as a potent political force and development partners[105]. Governments in developed countries thus recognize the fact that NGOs have become de facto partners in the establishment of global norms and standards, negotiating, influencing and proposing policy solutions to social problems like the spread of communicable diseases, poverty, housing and education crises, shrinking wages, ecosystems fragility, and human rights violations. These relationships established between the State and NGOs are described by Ebrahim (2005)

---

104   The American Enterprise Institute is a community of scholars and supporters committed to expanding liberty, increasing individual opportunity, and strengthening free enterprise. AEI pursues these unchanging ideals through independent thinking, open debate, reasoned argument, facts, and the highest standards of research and exposition. Without regard for politics or prevailing fashion, AEI dedicates its work to a more prosperous, safer, and more democratic nation and world. Retrieved from http://www.aei.org/

105   GPPi Research Project on Accountability in Global Governance. Retrieved from http://www.gppi.net/fileadmin/gppi/Jordan_Lisa_05022005.pdf

"as a set of unconnected binary relationships rather than as a system of relations". There is emphasis on all matters of strategic relevance and quantifiable metrics, particularly strategic planning, human resources and networking, and financial metrics, as the modus operandi of NGOs in many developed countries for long term social outcomes for clients and beneficiaries of services (Slim, 2002).

The universal appeal of OCL offers unlimited opportunities to NGOs in developing countries to build accountability relationships with international development partners and all stakeholders. With OCL, inappropriate models of accountability can be easily excluded and new OCL technologies such as Web 2.0 and social media tools are utilized to support ongoing learning dialogues among NGOs and programs stakeholders. OCL technological infrastructure is therefore a useful accountability tool for NGOs in developing countries. The successful incorporation and implementation of OCL technologies in the management systems of NGOs in developing countries build trust that facilitates acceptable social outcomes and improvements in the well-being of communities.

Accountability is the obligation to justify and explain conduct (Bovens, 2005, p. 6). In a for-profit organization, primary accountability is to shareholders of the company in the form of financial returns. All other stakeholders to a for-profit organization are considered secondary stakeholders and their needs are secondary to those of the shareholders. This represents a very traditional mercantile formula of accountability. The company represents the interests of the shareholders and its performance is measured in profit and growth. This mercantile tradition of accountability has roots in western capitalism but has now been challenged by progressive business people, NGOs and others who demand that corporate accountability become deeper and broader. Moving beyond a single financial 'bottom-line', companies are now being urged to account for a 'triple bottom-line' that also encompasses social and environmental accounting. Ethical business is thus being understood in terms of 'corporate citizenship' that makes companies explicitly responsible for wider 'public goods'. Their legitimacy increasingly depends on doing this or, at least, being seen to try to do it (Slim, 2002). "When you receive donations from the public, you have to not only be open, transparent and accountable; but you have to be able to demonstrate it" (Gibelman & Gelman, 2004).

NGOs, like organizations in the for-profit sector, are equally obligated to fulfill their accountability obligations. Many western NGOs have mainly been asked to report on the money raised and spent, the number of poor people reached, and the administrative cost of raising and spending the money. Fundraising and administration are often considered with peculiar benchmarks of organizational probity and efficiency in the voluntary sector. These areas have therefore attracted far greater scrutiny than the actual effect of the expenditure on poor people, which characterizes the fiscal focus of the protestant ethic and the spirit of capitalist charity.

NGOs can thus empower themselves in the manner in which commercial companies empower themselves, by being able to broaden and deepen their notion of accountability. Their legitimacy also depends on this. With NGO advocacy as a mainstream strategy in alleviating poverty and working for social justice, issues of accountability and legitimacy have become critical in recent years. NGOs speak out to challenge corporations, governments, armed factions and other non-state actors—staking out the key issues. Policy makers and thinkers understand this. To be credible and legitimate, NGOs are required to meet these two main requirements: First, they have to justify the voice with which they represent in their campaign materials, press conferences and private lobbying. Secondly, they have to prove the effectiveness of their programs—their authority emanating essentially from their presence and impact "in the field".

Chapter 5: Notions of Performance Accountability

Notions of performance accountability within the NGO community became serious in the 1990s, with high expectations for NGOs to be 'more accountable' for what they exist for. Well-founded criticisms of international NGOs' response to the Rwandan genocide created an environment in which humanitarian NGOs collaborated to put their industry in order by establishing several accountability mechanisms. These include:

- a Code of Conduct;
- a Humanitarian Charter and a set of technical standards called the Humanitarian Accountability Project (HAP)[106];
- a new emphasis on the quality and transparency of evaluations;
- an active learning network gathering and sharing the lessons learnt from humanitarian operations (ALNAP[107]), together with

---

106   Established in 2003, HAP International is the humanitarian sector's first international self-regulatory body. Members of HAP are committed to meeting the highest standards of accountability and quality management. In addition, HAP certifies those members that comply with the HAP Standard in Humanitarian Accountability and Quality Management, providing assurance to disaster survivors, staff, volunteers, host authorities and donors that the agency will deliver the best humanitarian service possible in each situation. Retrieved from http://www.hapinternational.org/default. aspx

107   The Active Learning Network for Accountability and Performance in Humanitarian Action (ALNAP) was established in 1997, following the multi-agency evaluation of the Rwanda genocide. ALNAP is a collective response by the humanitarian sector, dedicated to improving humanitarian performance through increased learning and accountability. A unique network, ALNAP incorporates many of the key humanitarian organizations and experts from across the humanitarian sector. Members are drawn from donors, NGOs, the Red Cross/Crescent, the UN, independents and aca-

- initiatives to explore quality models and professional accreditation.

Many NGOs came to realize that they too have a multiple bottom-line to achieve in their development work. It became unacceptable to simply report in terms of program 'outputs' like a well dug or the distribution of a ton of improved seed. 'Outcome' monitoring and 'impact' assessment became essential methods in NGOs' purposes of existence. The practice of social audit also became quite relevant in NGO work in the same manner social and environmental audit became a burden on commercial corporations. Most international NGOs also adopted strategic planning and logical framework analysis that enabled them to set specific objectives across their organizations (from board level to project level) and account for them like corporations. Most NGOs, however, have found that profit or outputs are much easier to show than providing answers to the more difficult questions of outcome, impact and attribution; which makes the current art and science of social and environmental accounting truly complex on occasion. Accounting for the impact or outcome of NGO work can be uncertain, is usually contested and can border on pure speculation at times as NGOs try to track cause and effect between their actions and the personal, social, economic, environmental and political change around their projects.

Accountability mechanisms on many government funded NGO programs, with 'upward and external' dimensions of accountability, are sometimes seen as overly bureaucratic with an overly procedural mindset that undermine NGOs' missions and its mandates on provision of services (McGregor-Lowndes & Ryan, 2009). But this should not be confused with the essence of organizational definitions of quality: a commitment to continuous improvement and a core set of key organizational standards. NGO managers and officers have a vital role in

---

demics. ALNAP uses the broad range of experience and expertise within its membership to produce tools and analysis relevant and accessible to the humanitarian sector as a whole. ALNAP's work plan is aimed at improving humanitarian performance through learning and accountability, and consists of core activities, project activities and linked activities. Retrieved from http://www.alnap.org/

the success of any development organization, especially in the realm of community perception of quality. To communities, "quality" means how well coordinated a service was provided, not how technically superior the actual service or development component turned out. This definition of quality can also be referred to as program or development impact on community. An NGO can therefore develop quality processes geared toward community expectations by doing a number of things, including the following:

- clear identification of outcomes, and empowerment of project staff to achieve goals;
- formation of an integrated quality development team to establish quality metrics;
- recognizing cultural competences which can be built into quality processes; and
- aligning the organization's mission to the overall quality program.

With a successful quality program, an NGO can expect a considerable return on fiscal commitments, satisfied development staff, and improved development outcomes.

Quality is the core of a development organization's excellence. A focus on quality is any development organization's management's responsibility to ensure that quality processes are followed throughout the organization. Such excellence is determined by the communities' perceptions and impact of a program. Drivers of development impact are not development factors. Instead, they relate to project objectives met and responsiveness of development staff and providers, including appropriate use of development funds, project impact, and ability to collaborate with other development actors. Ultimately, this satisfaction feeds into improved development quality. Of course, development excellence also contributes to total community development, but reaching out to the greater community can make up for complications in the technicalities of the program that are sometimes unavoidable.

Accreditation Accountability

Also tied to the definition of quality is accreditation. NGO accreditation demonstrates that the overall satisfaction of beneficiaries has a role in determining the value of providers. Accreditation has become an integral part of continuous readiness efforts of NGOs to drive sustained improvement in countries they operate. It is simply a validation process by which institutions of development work are evaluated against established standards. There are global, regional, as well as national agencies involved in the accreditation process of NGOs. In most cases, the role that governments play is to evaluate these accrediting agencies using well developed criteria in order to identify those considered to be "reliable authorities" on the quality and capabilities of NGOs.

The following is a list of some of the major accreditation agencies in various parts of the world:

- The Joint Commission and the National Committee for Quality Assurance[108], is a US based institution whose accreditation is focused on patients' safety and better quality outcomes.
- The Council for Higher Education Accreditation (CHEA)[109], also a US-based institution, accredits accreditation agencies. Recognition by CHEA affirms that the standards and processes of the accrediting organization

---

108   An independent, not-for-profit organization, The Joint Commission accredits and certifies more than 18,000 health care organizations and programs in the United States. Joint Commission accreditation and certification is recognized nationwide as a symbol of quality that reflects an organization's commitment to meeting certain performance standards. Retrieved from http://www.jointcommission.org/AboutUs/

109   Council for Higher Education Accreditation...*Accreditation Serving the Public Interest*. A national advocate and institutional voice for self-regulation of academic quality through accreditation, CHEA is an association of 3,000 degree-granting colleges and universities and recognizes 60 institutional and programmatic accrediting organizations. Retrieved from http://www.chea.org/

are consistent with the academic quality, improvement and accountability expectations that CHEA has established. Also, the Department of Education is making available a searchable database of postsecondary institutions and programs accredited by accrediting agencies or state approval agencies recognized by the U.S. Secretary of Education.

- The Department of Public Information (DPI) of the United Nations[110], established since 1947, maintains official relationships between DPI and NGOs dating back to 1968. The Economic and Social Council[111] in its resolution 1297 called on DPI to associate NGOs with effective information programs in place and thus dis-

---

110   The Department of Public Information (DPI) was established in 1946 by General Assembly resolution 13 (1). As the public voice of the United Nations, DPI promotes global awareness and greater understanding of the work of the United Nations, using various communication tools including radio, television, print, the Internet, videoconferencing and increasingly other new information technology. Retrieved from http://unic.un.org/aroundworld/unics/en/whoWeAre/aboutDPI/index.asp

111   ECOSOC was established under the United Nations Charter as the principal organ to coordinate economic, social, and related work of the 14 UN specialized agencies, functional commissions and five regional commissions. The Council also receives reports from 11 UN funds and programs. The Economic and Social Council (ECOSOC) serves as the central forum for discussing international economic and social issues, and for formulating policy recommendations addressed to Member States and the United Nations system. It is responsible for: promoting higher standards of living, full employment, and economic and social progress; identifying solutions to international economic, social and health problems; facilitating international cultural and educational cooperation; and encouraging universal respect for human rights and fundamental freedoms. It has the power to make or initiate studies and reports on these issues. It also has the power to assist the preparations and organization of major international conferences in the economic and social and related fields and to facilitate a coordinated follow-up to these conferences. With its broad mandate the Council's purview extends to over 70 per cent of the human and financial resources of the entire UN system. Retrieved from http://www.un.org/en/ecosoc/

seminate information about issues on the UN's agenda and the work of the Organization. Through associated NGOs, DPI seeks to reach people around the world and help them better understand the work and aims of the United Nations.

- The United Nations Non-Governmental Liaison Service (UN-NGLS)[112] is an inter-agency program of the United Nations mandated to promote and develop constructive relations between the UN and civil society organizations.

- AusAid[113], the Australia-based agency's accreditation process aims to provide AusAID, and the Australian public, with confidence that the Australian Government is funding professional, well managed, community based organizations that are capable of delivering quality development outcomes. Accreditation acts as a front-end risk management process and ensures

---

112   The United Nations Non-Governmental Liaison Service (NGLS) promotes constructive relations between the United Nations and civil society through dynamic partnerships to foster greater coherence around cross-cutting and emerging issues on the UN's agenda and by facilitating meaningful civil society engagement in UN processes. Drawing on its inter-agency nature and UN system-wide perspective, NGLS provides strategic information, analysis and support to a wide range of constituencies, using its unique convening and networking capacity to strengthen multi-stakeholder dialogue and alliance-building on core UN issues. Retrieved from http://www.un-ngls.org/spip.php?page=sommaire

113   AusAID is the Australian Government agency responsible for managing Australia's overseas aid program. The objective of the aid program is to assist developing countries reduce poverty and achieve sustainable development, in line with Australia's national interest. AusAID provides advice and support to the Minister and Parliamentary Secretary on development policy, and plans and coordinates poverty reduction activities in partnership with developing countries. AusAID's head office is in Canberra. AusAID also has representatives in 37 Australian diplomatic missions overseas. Retrieved from http://www.ausaid.gov.au/default.cfm

accountable use of funding with minimal activity overview by AusAID.

- Alliance[114] is providing a new system of international accreditation, building on the work of national monitoring bodies over many years by keeping tabs on multinational NGOs. The objects of the charity are to promote the efficiency and effectiveness of charities and the effective use of charitable resources for the public benefit by publishing journals, reports and other material relating to the administration and effectiveness of charities and the effective use of charitable resources; and convening discussion and dialogue on these issues.

- The United Nations Department of Economic and Social Affairs (DESA) NGO Branch[115] is the focal point within the UN Secretariat for non-governmental organizations in consultative status with the Economic

---

114   Alliance is the leading magazine for philanthropy and social investment worldwide. It provides news and analysis of what's happening in the philanthropy and social investment sectors across the world. It also acts as a forum for exchange of ideas and experiences among practitioners. Retrieved from http://www.alliancemagazine.org/

115   The United Nations Department of Economic and Social Affairs (DESA) and its predecessors have helped countries around the world meet their economic, social and environmental challenges for more than 50 years. DESA's mission—to promote development for all—reflects a fundamental concern for equity and equality in countries large and small, developed and developing. Within the framework of the United Nations Development Agenda, DESA works on issues ranging from poverty reduction, population, gender equality and indigenous rights to macroeconomic policy, development finance, public sector innovation, forest policy, climate change and sustainable development. The Department also supports the effort to achieve the Millennium Development Goals, a set of time-bound targets, which put the eradication of poverty at the centre of the global partnership for development. At the United Nations, DESA provides the substantive support to intergovernmental processes on development issues in the General Assembly and in the Economic and Social Council, its functional commissions and expert bodies. https://www.un.org/en/development/desa/about/index.shtml

and Social Council (ECOSOC) and for NGOs seeking status. The NGO Branch services the Committee on Non-Governmental Organizations, a subsidiary body of the ECOSOC composed of 19 Member States. It also provides relevant advice and information concerning NGOs to representatives of the United Nations system, Member States and civil society. The Branch works to strengthen and enhance dialogue between NGOs and the United Nations to enable NGOs to participate in the economic and social development activities of the organization.

- Credibility Alliance[116] is a consortium of voluntary organizations committed towards enhancing accountability and transparency in the voluntary sector through good governance. It is a professional body based in India that sets norms and standards of governance in the voluntary sector.

- The British Overseas Aid Group (BOAG), consisting of the five biggest international NGOs in the UK provides standards and quality frameworks in the UK voluntary sector. The BOAG explores the idea of quality standards in development work.

Most international NGOs also now pursue a quality and standards approach. World Vision International[117] has ten 'ministry standards' for

---

116   Credibility Alliance is a consortium of voluntary organizations committed towards enhancing accountability and transparency in the voluntary sector through good governance. It is an initiative that emerged from within the sector and was registered in May 2004 as an independent, not-for-profit organization after an extensive consultative process over a period of two years involving thousands of voluntary organizations all over India. As an organization CA aspires to build trust among all stakeholders through improving governance with in the voluntary sector. Credibility Alliance is akin to a professional body that will set norms or standards of governance. Retrieved from http://www.credall.org.in/index.htm

117   World Vision is a Christian humanitarian organization dedicated to

its 65 member agencies. Oxfam International has developed common program standards among its 11 organizations, and Caritas International[118] has begun its own attempt to set quality standards across its many member organizations. The Ford Foundation[119] has in place the 'light but firm' quality standards for NGOs, an independent development Ombudsman, certification and agreed complaints procedures.

There are, however, risks of excessive bureaucracy involved with such elaborate standardized rules of engagement in development work. The world of development is about relationships and partnerships between NGOs and target beneficiaries. An overly business-like application of quality and standards could therefore distort such relationships which could be counter-productive because excessive bureaucratic processes destroy motivation. Besides, there is the tendency for mission-driven workers to lose interest and an atmosphere of fear prevailing in which organizations forsake their primary objectives, i.e. responsiveness and flexibility, in their struggle to retain funding (Brown & Troutt, 2007, p. 222). Functional funding agreements could be acceptable alternatives as instruments of downward and internal mechanisms of accountability (Flack & Ryan, 2005, p. 75). The important work of the International Non-Governmental Organizations Accountability Charter[120], the

---

working with children, families, and their communities worldwide to reach their full potential by tackling the causes of poverty and injustice. Retrieved from http://www.worldvision.org/

118   The eradication of poverty and social inequality lies at the very core of what Caritas does. Caritas provides assistance to the most vulnerable on behalf of Catholics around the world. Retrieved from http://www.caritas.org/

119   The Ford Foundation is committed to tackling enduring problems that require sustained effort and resolve. The foundation is governed by a 14-member board of trustees, which includes our president. Our grant making program is led by directors and regional representatives who work with a talented cadre of program officers. Retrieved from http://www.fordfoundation.org/

120   The INGO Accountability Charter provides a recognized standard for good governance for NGOs. It complements the World YWCA Standards of Good Management and Accountability and Internal Control System and has become an integral part of our annual governance and review process.

NGO-Watch[121], and the One World Trust[122], is work in the right direction to improve context-specific accountability mechanisms in developing countries, that should also take into consideration the geographical and cultural circumstances of NGOs.

Voice Accountability

Accountability for what NGOs represent is another important trend, also known as 'voice accountability' which goes to determine the key matters of NGO legitimacy and credibility. The empirical veracity of what NGOs represent, and the political authority with which they take a position, however, remain tested. Today, though most international NGOs have their foundations on experience-based advocacy, these INGOs are increasing their research capacity by forging strategic alliances with academics and think tanks to guarantee quality in their position statements.

Pro-poor NGOs should focus on how their voice relates to the people they are primarily concerned about: the poor, people whose rights are

Retrieved from http://www.ingoaccountabilitycharter.org/

121   Global Governance Watch® (GGW) is a joint project of the American Enterprise Institute (AEI) and the Federalist Society for Law and Public Policy Studies. Its goal is to raise awareness about global governance, to monitor how international organizations influence domestic political outcomes, and to address issues of transparency and accountability within the United Nations, related intergovernmental organizations (IGOs), and other non-state actors. Retrieved from http://www.globalgovernancewatch.org/ngo_watch/

122   Global Governance Watch® (GGW) is a joint project of the American Enterprise Institute (AEI) and the Federalist Society for Law and Public Policy Studies. Its goal is to raise awareness about global governance, to monitor how international organizations influence domestic political outcomes, and to address issues of transparency and accountability within the United Nations, related intergovernmental organizations (IGOs), and other non-state actors.

Retrieved from http://www.globalgovernancewatch.org/ngo_watch/

violated, and the victims of war. When NGOs *'speak as'* the poor, *'with'* the poor, *'for'* the poor or *'about'* the poor, they endeavour to guarantee credibility and legitimacy. They *'speak as'* based on the characteristics of the target beneficiaries they represent, be they the poor or victims of human rights violations. They *'speak with'* when NGOs work closely with their target groups and speaks with their consent. They can claim to *'speak for'* or on behalf of, when the poor and oppressed they represent are unable to speak out for themselves. And when NGOs are not strictly *'speaking as'*, *'with'* or *'for'* a particular group of poor or victimised people, or are speaking so generally as to make specific relationships meaningless, then they may claim to be *'speaking about'* poverty or oppression.

OCL tools and methodologies are empowering non-profit civil society organizations globally to support communities around the world on social, environmental, education and health issues. For example, the International HIV/AIDS Alliance[123] shares a vision of a world in which people do not die of AIDS. The alliance commits to a growing global partnership for community action and aim to provide strength to each other through its work. Through collaboration across the Alliance members can each learn faster, expand quality programming, and provide more effective responses that make a difference to the lives of those living with or affected by HIV.

OCL relationship to voice accountability of NGOs is evidenced in the work of NGOs collaborating to provide more powerful voice for change, greater access to national and international forums, and a reputation built around professionalism, technical expertise and sustainability. NGOs become empowered by using OCL tools to provide strength and support to each other in pursuit of their common goals and objectives. NGOs can use these tools to outline their common commitment to

---

123   The International HIV/AIDS Alliance (The Alliance) is an innovative global partnership of civil society organizations and an international secretariat working to support community action on AIDS. The Alliance is committed to strengthening communities' abilities to influence HIV policies at both a global and national level. Retrieved from http://www. aidsalliance.org/

excellence, transparency and accountability. NGOs can demonstrate and build on their:

- commitments to support the development of policy positions on key issues;
- promote transparency, accountability and good governance;
- improve their performance and effectiveness as organizations;
- help build stronger alliances through their words and actions;
- share information and knowledge to strengthen the voices of their organization; and
- support fundraising opportunities of mutual benefit.

By all accounts of OCL capacity, voice accountability of NGOs offers possibilities into best practices of organizational capacity building among national and international development organizations working in partnership. In the past decade, even oppressive political institutions that once seem impenetrable and insurmountable by common citizens have crumbled in humanity's path of capable OCL communication and information technologies, and a breathtaking array of new organizational arrangements in grassroots organizations, social movements, global networks, collaborative alliances, public-private partnerships, and socially responsible businesses. Perhaps, never before in the history of humankind has there been a period of such expansive, social, cultural and institutional change on a global scale as there is today. The centrality of organizations to humankind's common global future is but one of many important forces driving the voice accountability conversation of NGOs. Any effort to understand, let alone implement significant human-scale development must include a sustained commitment to improving knowledge and practice of organizational capacity building. There is wide recognition that healthy, vibrant organizations and institutions are central to a sustainable world future, and there is a renewed commitment to include all voices and experimental strategies in advancing broad scale human development. Technologies can provide greater efficiency in managing information or serve to improve the quality of the information used to guide the voice accountability systems of NGOs.

By far, the greatest use of technology is to serve the efficiency functions—communication by email, Web sites, data storage and statistical manipulations and distributing record keeping and analytical functions using statistical packages and spreadsheets. There are also efficiencies attributable to search and comparison functions, where NGO practitioners can access information, especially on issues relevant to their missions. While the access to digital material is faster, browser technology in OCL mechanisms also adds value by suggesting options that might otherwise go unexplained. It is central, however, for NGOs and human rights groups to be clear about where their voice comes from in a given situation and to be transparent about it. Their legitimacy is thus brought to bear depending on their voice or who and what they represent.

Chapter 6: Sources of Legitimacy

Legitimacy and accountability are not the same, but they are closely related. Legitimacy is defined as *'the particular status with which an organization is imbued and perceived at any given time that enables it to operate with the general consent of peoples, governments, companies and non-state groups around the world*"[124]. An NGO or human rights group's legitimacy is both *derived* and *generated*. It is derived from morality and law. It is generated by veracity, tangible support and more intangible goodwill[125].

Claiming the prerogative to speak out basically because an NGO has ongoing projects is improbably to be satisfactory to a cynical constituency in the media, among other observers, and—most importantly—a more critical local population. Southern NGOs are quizzical about the prerogative of Northern NGOs to speak for them; women are often suspect of male-dominated NGOs to represent them; and as access to technology grows, communities feel they can speak for themselves through video and the internet as well as more traditional arenas such as marches and demonstrations. As more people globally discover less costly ways to access information and find a louder voice in global debates, the superseding authority of northern-based, male-dominated organizations to appropriate the voices of others will ebb away completely. What is becoming of the world today is more and more sharing of technological resources, and access to power, in more democratic networks.

NGOs have to be competent and dependable civic actors themselves—otherwise they will be restrained in encouraging co-operation and accountability in other institutions—nor will they be considered legitimate players in a talented international civil society. However, only some NGOs have genuinely democratic systems of governance or accountability so far. As social actors they certainly need such democratic systems in place, even though as service providers they can do without them. The authority of a social actor comes from their

---

124   SUR: International Journal of Human Rights, 2009
125   Slim, 2002

entrenched commitment to their own society, from a more betrothed and supportive domestic constituency, and from the alliances they build up with other parts of civil society. NGOs will have to become more open and transparent in an age when institutional accountability is a condition for a seat at the negotiating table. The practice of concealing contentious issues, and the deliberate failure to convert NGO rhetoric about equity and participatory management into institutional practice, is hardly a good basis for persuading others of the need for reform. If NGOs are to become social actors in a global world—pushing for justice, equity, democracy and accountability—then clearly these characteristics need to be reflected in their own systems and structures.

Moral and Legal Basis of Legitimacy

NGOs are essentially self-mandating, not governed by any specific mandates given to them by states under international law. Their legality and their moral recognition are more grounded on principles than on specific international statutes. Nonetheless, NGOs gain legitimacy by claiming their legality within international law and by being law-abiding, operating within governments' legislations. Internationally, NGOs claim legitimacy by being governed by Article 71 of the UN Charter with reference to human rights law, international humanitarian law and refugee law. Under international humanitarian law, the staffs of NGOs are recognised as protected persons in an armed conflict. Such protection accorded NGO operators as protected persons in armed conflicts increases the legitimacy of NGOs.

The 1986 General Assembly Declaration on the Right to Development makes clear that 'all human beings have a responsibility for development—individually and collectively'. Building on this principle of responsibility, the UN General Assembly also adopted a specific Declaration on Human Rights Defenders in 1998 that affirms the right of individuals and groups to promote and protect human rights. The moral foundations of an NGO's legitimacy are equally important. An organisational mission to challenge and end human rights violations is derived from a moral basis grounded on the values of human equality, dignity, impartiality, justice, freedom and personal and collective responsibility. This moral foundation gives human rights organisations and NGOs a principled legitimacy that reverberates with the moral reasoning of peoples globally. Expression and recognition of this fundamental morality is essential to an organisation's legitimacy, the lack of which as with the case of such organizations like the Ku Klux Klan[126] in the United States and many other hate groups and gangs around the world, which are distinctly uncivil in their missions and values, cannot claim moral legitimacy.

Tangible and Intangible Basis of Legitimacy

Legitimacy derived legally and morally from principles can also be engendered tangibly and intangibly in practice. An organisation's most tangible structure of legitimacy comes in the form of direct support from its sponsors and the people it seeks to help. The consent of the people it seeks to help and the representative membership of an NGO go a long way to enhance the legitimacy of an NGO. NGO support with financial contributions from sponsors is another source of popular and official legitimacy. Oxfam, for instance, receives contributions from over 600,000 monthly givers and other sporadic givers, including governments. The massive voluntary support Oxfam also gets is as well a hugely important source of legitimacy. All these are tangible assets of support made manifest in money, time and intellectual agreement and

---

126   Ku Klux Klan, often abbreviated KKK and informally known as The Klan, is the name of three distinct past and present far-right organizations in the United States, which have advocated extremist reactionary currents such as white supremacy, white nationalism, and anti-immigration, historically expressed through terrorism. Since the mid-20th century, the KKK has also been anti-communist. The current manifestation is splintered into several chapters and is classified as a hate group. Retrieved from http://en.wikipedia.org/wiki/Ku_Klux_Klan

shared conviction. Such tangible support systems become more sacrosanct when linked to real and transparent accountability mechanisms. Informed consent of an NGO's activities when supporters and target beneficiaries are properly informed about its work, especially how monies are used and program impact, reinforces legitimacy.

Tangible Relationships, Knowledge and Performance

Knowledge and relationships are other forms of legitimacy. Having profound expertise on a subject, such as human rights law and human rights violations, is a major source of legitimacy. And connections with the power brokers—the politicians, the military leaders and TNC s—give organizations legitimate contacts and a tangible source of legitimacy. Legitimacy is also generated by a performing NGO that delivers on its promises and enabling real benefits and the peoples it serves. When an NGO concept works in practice it becomes a more legitimate enterprise. Well-rounded performance (especially performance that resonates with the values of human rights) is therefore sources of legitimacy.

Intangible Sources of Trust, Integrity and Reputation

Qualities such as credibility, reputation, trust and integrity are key to an organisation's legitimacy. These are the intangible aspects of an NGO's legitimacy—when people are able to trust an organization and believe in its work, gives legitimacy to that organization. These are the 'goodwill' intangible qualities of an organization, better described by the classicists as an organization's 'aura' or the established 'kudos' of an agency which are equally important.

Methods of Accountability

An operational definition of NGO accountability involves the three aspects of reporting, involving and responding. NGO accountability is therefore '*the process by which an NGO holds itself openly responsible for what it believes, what it does, and what it does not do, for all concerned parties to get involved and responding to what it learns*'. Accountability is a process and it is about utilizing creative mechanisms used to measure an NGO's purpose and impact. In a special issue of the Institute of Development Studies (IDS)[127] Bulletin on "*Accountability through Participation*," Cornwall, Lucas, and Pasteur (2000, p.3) broaden this perspective by suggesting that accountability is both about being "held responsible" by others and about "taking responsibility" for oneself. The most common accountability mechanisms available include:

- *Social audits*: The methodology of social auditing is a management tool organizations use to review and demonstrate their social, economic, and environmental benefits and limitations. Social audits are ways of taking account of the extent to which organizations live up to their shared values and objectives; and can be used for marketing, promotion and advocacy purposes. Social audits involve stakeholders (i.e. employees, clients, volunteers, funders, contractors, suppliers and the community) in providing systematic and regular assessments of the impact of an organization's non-financial objectives. Social audits balance organizations' annual financial audits by providing clear and succinct information on performance against social objectives. The process of social auditing requires an intermittent but clear time

---

127   The IDS vision is a world in which poverty does not exist, social justice prevails and sustainable growth promotes human wellbeing. IDS is home to approximately 100 researchers, 70 knowledge services staff, 65 support staff and about 150 students at any one time.
Retrieved from http://www.ids.ac.uk/go/home

commitment from key persons within the organizations who liaise with others in the organization and designs, co-ordinates, analyses and documents the information collected during the process. With social auditing information is collected through research methods that include social bookkeeping, surveys and case studies in accordance with objectives of organizations as starting point from which indicators of impact are determined (Kumar & Sharma, 2005). The results are fed into the organizations' strategic review and planning processes to improve overall performance and social impact.

- Designing the social audit methodology is time consuming and involves providing training and support to auditors within the organization. The Northern Ireland Open College Network[128] is accredited for having developed a social auditing approach being adapted by many non-governmental organizations. A detailed training manual has also been produced and can be obtained from the Northern Ireland Social Economy Agency.[129]

- *Evaluations*: Creating a more effective system for the evaluation and regulation of social groups has become increasingly important. An efficient and proven NGO evaluation system in terms of impact assessments of development interventions is a major contribution to the establishment of a new NGO management system in developing countries. It involves reviewing currently

---

128   OCN Northern Ireland is committed to the idea that learning is a lifelong experience and is further committed to supporting that learning journey for all. OCN Northern Ireland endeavors to create and sustain partnership that add value to its network; build relationships that help to create learning communities; and championing learning rights. Retrieved from http://www.ocnni.org.uk

129   The Social Economy Network is a membership-based organization that draws its membership from social economy organizations throughout Northern Ireland. Retrieved from http://www.socialeconomyagency.org

employed definitions of impact and of impact assessment; and understanding the main difficulties in relation to the development of an appropriate methodology for impact assessment: the confusion between the evaluation of a project's objectives and an assessment of its long-term impact; the often poor development of evaluation tools and methodologies and the complexity of assessing impact qualitatively.

- *External Regulation*: External regulation means intelligent regulation in terms of engaging with NGOs in a reciprocal way that will make most difference to them and those who benefit from them. At the heart of an effective approach lies the concept that regulation is all about helping people to do things better themselves. Effective regulation is not limited to regulatory action taken by Governments. There are four essential components of effective regulation each of which are equally important in enabling NGOs to carry out their vital work effectively. These are:

  o *Legal framework*—working towards an enabling legal environment, which supports effective regulation and protects the operating space of NGOs.

  o *Regulation*—supports the development of effective, proportionate NGO regulation.

  o *Government/sector dialogue*—supports the environment and mechanisms conducive to the development of a co-operative and mutually respectful relationship between government and NGOs

  o *Sector capacity*—ensures that the sector has the skills and capacity necessary to create and maintain a healthy, accountable and independent NGO sector.

NGOs should engage in each of these areas as they work with civil society and government bodies across the world to contribute to healthy, independent and accountable NGO sectors.

- *Use of Complaints Procedures*: NGOs commonly employ intergovernmental mechanisms to seek a universal remedy for a violation or to pressure a government to cease activities which violate, or could violate, human rights. Inter-governmental complaint procedures require that domestic remedies be exhausted before engaging an international mechanism. This can include demonstrating that no domestic remedies exist. Corporate Social Responsibility (CSR) standard-setting, reporting and monitoring institutions have evolved and matured through time, and complaints procedures are gradually being developed. There is also now in place an external review procedure for the "*Communications on Progress*[130]" that a company must submit.

Again, today, there is the ability of victims of corporate wrong-doing to use the existing regulatory or legal infrastructure to settle disputes and seek redress. This is occurring in countries such as the United States and the United Kingdom where cases have been brought against companies for wrongs committed abroad, or in India through Public

---

130   The United Nations Global Compact Communication on Progress booklet is intended to provide Global Compact participants with inspiration and ideas on how to communicate progress in implementing the ten principles. It is the result of an ongoing dialogue between the Global Compact Office and many of our participating companies. In particular, it reflects experiences and perspectives shared by practitioners and users of Communications on Progress (COPs). Retrieved from http://www.unglobalcompact.org/docs/communication_on_progress/4.3/leading_the_way.pdf

Interest Litigation[131]. The Aarhus Convention[132] allows NGOs in countries that host TNCs to obtain information about their environmental performance.

Methods of managing and mobilizing associated with "transnational" or "multi-scalar" activism, which entail connecting organizations and networks at local, national, regional and international levels, are on the whole important, and have played a crucial role in efforts to bring to court corporate wrong-doing, as well as in campaigns where activists "name and shame" companies. Civil society organizations, working at diverse levels, are now also increasingly obliged to reconnect with local and national governments, to develop complementarities and synergies in regulatory capacity.

---

131   In Indian law, public interest litigation means litigation for the protection of the public interest. It is litigation introduced in a court of law, not by the aggrieved party but by the court itself or by any other private party. It is not necessary, for the exercise of the court's jurisdiction, that the person who is the victim of the violation of his or her right should personally approach the court. Public interest litigation is the power given to the public by courts through judicial activism. However, the person filing the petition must prove to the satisfaction of the court that the petition is being filed for a public interest and not just as a frivolous litigation by a busy body. Such cases may occur when the victim does not have the necessary resources to commence litigation or his freedom to move court has been suppressed or encroached upon. The court can itself take cognizance of the matter and proceed *suo motu* or cases can commence on the petition of any public-spirited individual. Retrieved from http://en.wikipedia.org/wiki/Public_Interest_Litigation

132   The UNECE Convention on Access to Information, Public Participation in Decision-Making and Access to Justice in Environmental Matters was adopted on 25th June 1998 in the Danish city of Aarhus at the Fourth Ministerial Conference in the 'Environment for Europe' process. The Aarhus Convention is a new kind of environmental agreement. The Convention: links environmental rights and human rights, acknowledges that we owe an obligation to future generations, establishes that sustainable development can be achieved only through the involvement of all stakeholders, links government accountability and environmental protection, focuses on interactions between the public and public authorities in a democratic context. Retrieved from http://www.unece.org/env/pp/

Other possibilities of activism may include expanding the remit of the International Criminal Court[133] to address corporate crimes; as well as setting up new UN activities including institutions information systems on corporate accountability initiatives and laws, and on business practices associated with mal-development; new institutions such as a Special Rapporteur on TNCs, or a Corporate Accountability Convention[134] or Organization; the (re)chartering and down-sizing of corporations; a set of Civil Society Rules for TNCs; or even revisiting the principle of limited liability. NGOs and trade unions can also now operationalize or activate complaints procedures such as those that exist at least on paper in the OECD Guidelines on Multinational Corporations[135].

- *Use of NGO Alternative Reports*: NGO "alternative" reports as a way of vetting information provided in governments' periodic reports are now often used by some intergovernmental bodies, such as the Committee

---

133   The International Criminal Court (ICC), governed by the Rome Statute, is the first permanent, treaty based, international criminal court established to help end impunity for the perpetrators of the most serious crimes of concern to the international community. The ICC is an independent international organization, and is not part of the United Nations system. Its seat is at The Hague in the Netherlands. Although the Court's expenses are funded primarily by States Parties, it also receives voluntary contributions from governments, international organizations, individuals, corporations and other entities. Retrieved from http://www.icc-cpi.int/Menus/ICC/Home

134   Corporate Accountability >> Documents and Publications >> CSR, Codes of Conduct & Voluntary Initiatives http://www.corporate-accountability.org/eng/documents_and_publications/

135   OECD Guidelines on Multinational Corporations: The Guidelines are recommendations addressed by governments to multinational enterprises operating in or from adhering countries (the OECD members plus Argentina, Brazil and Chile). They provide voluntary principles and standards for responsible business conduct, in a variety of areas including employment and industrial relations, human rights, environment, information disclosure, competition, taxation, and science and technology (see *The OECD Guidelines for Multinational Enterprises: Chapters*). Retrieved from http://www.oecd.org/dataoecd/12/21/1903291.pdf

on Economic, Social and Cultural Rights and the Committee on the Rights of the Child. Activists and organizations may use NGO Alternative Reports as reporting processes to alert governments that their actions are being monitored by organizations within their countries, to solicit attention to and seek remedies for given violations, or to clarify the nature and extent of governments' obligations with regard to given rights. NGOs can develop a general alternative report following the guidelines given to states parties for the development of periodic reports, and can fill in gaps where the government has not reported on certain problems or point to a lack of appropriate government action[136].

- *Membership Systems*: Membership systems are an effective accountability mechanism for NGOs based on democratic governance structures intended to provide both internal accountability (leaders are elected) and external legitimacy (leaders represent their constituencies). In terms of external roles, membership that is sufficiently homogeneous along key dimensions (poverty, occupation, gender, etc), can be instrumental in framing issues, generating policy-relevant information, leverag-

---

136   In 1995 the Colombian Commission of Jurists (CCJ) submitted an alternative report to the CESCR in coordination with other Colombian NGOs. The CCJ obtained a copy of the government's initial report submitted to the CESCR's inter-sessional working group. Based on their review of the initial report, the NGOs developed a list of 80-85 questions related to gaps they identified or inaccuracies in the governmental information, and submitted this list to the CESCR working group. From this list, the working group posed around 40 questions to the government. The NGOs also used these questions as a guideline for writing their alternative report, which was submitted in Spanish. The CCJ sent a 10-page summary of the report in English to the non-Spanish-speaking members of the Committee. In addition, it developed a 4-page summary of the report which was accepted by the UN as an official document and thus was translated into all of the UN working languages by UN services. Retrieved from http://www1.umn.edu/humanrts/edumat/IHRIP/ripple/chapter7.html

ing policy reform, and otherwise mediating the external environment. Members can also help leverage contacts, power, and influence. The role of membership dues, in cash and kind, is significant. And a strongly internalized "code of moral conduct" that guides actions of the organization and of individuals in the organization also keeps leadership accountable to members. There are a good number of membership management software and social networking platforms available today to support NGO work that can be found on resourceful platforms such as DownV[137], with downloadable programs that allow NGOs to keep accurate and up-to-date membership records online, creating mailings, among other features. YourMembership.Com,[138] a provider of SaaS-model online member communities, for instance, offers web-based membership management software plus social networking features as a complete online member community.

- *Environmental Impact Assessments (EIAs)*: The rationale of EIAs is to guarantee that decision makers reflect on the consequent environmental impacts when contem-

---

137   DownV is the free resource of NGO membership management software download. Retrieved from http://www.downv.com/Linux-software-download/NGO-membership

138   YourMembership.com allows organizations to easily control the features of their online member community, while delivering integrated enterprise-level membership management software for greater operational efficiencies... no matter the level of technical expertise. Best of all, there's no hardware to purchase, confusing software to install, or future upgrade costs. The flexibility of YourMembership.com web-based (SaaS-model) solution allows organizations to tailor it to their organization's specific needs, and as their needs grow they can tap into the additional features YourMembership.com has to offer without the worry of additional cost. YourMembership.com's web 2.0 online communities and membership management software solutions include: custom design, all features, hosting, future upgrades, customer service and training. Retrieved from http://www.yourmembership.com/

plating on whether to proceed with a project. The International Association for Impact Assessment (IAIA)[139], the leading global network on best practice in the use of impact assessment for informed decision-making regarding policies, programs, plans and projects, has defined an environmental impact assessment as "the process of identifying, predicting, evaluating and mitigating the biophysical, social, and other relevant effects of development proposals prior to major decisions being taken and commitments made". EIAs are distinctive in that they do not necessitate patronage to a pre-ordained environmental outcome, but rather they lead decision-makers to account for environmental values in their decisions and to justify those decisions in light of detailed environmental studies and public comments on the potential environmental impacts of the proposal. The IAIA has developed the *Preliminary Index of Useful Internet Web Sites*[140] as a compilation of Internet Web sites that are related to environmental assessment.

- *Specific Stakeholder Surveys*: Stakeholders are a significant resource. Engaging them constructively is fundamental to securing their loyalty, commitment and sup-

---

139   The International Association for Impact Assessment exists to improve and better inform the decision-making of today that has environmental consequences for tomorrow. IAIA is a multi-disciplinary organization for environmental practitioners and interested participants from all sectors: government, industry, training, research, consultancies and community bases. A primary purpose of IAIA is developing international and local capacity to make wise decisions regarding the anticipation, management and planning of environmental change. Considering ecological and human consequences is essential to enhance the quality of life for all. Retrieved from http://www.iaia.org/default.aspx

140   The *Preliminary Index of Useful Websites* has been prepared by Tamara Herman, Fiona Barker, Hilary Clark and Peter Croal for the Environmental Assessment and Compliance Unit of the Canadian International Development Agency (CIDA). Retrieved from http://www.iaia.org/resources-networking/eia-index-of-websites.aspx

port. Engagement is a foremost objective and advantage of nonprofit planning; as such planned surveys must be carefully constructed and analyzed. Reporting back to the participants about voices heard, as well as lessons learned and actions taken from them, is key to an organization's obligations to its stakeholders, rather increasing all sense of transparency and responsiveness. While there are several reasons for being obliged to conduct a stakeholder survey, at the core of all is clearly a desire to recognize and serve all stakeholders better. The Applied Corporate Governance™[141] methodology offers a stakeholder survey based on the Five Golden Rules[142] of good corporate governance. The OECD Principles of Corporate Governance[143] states: "*Corporate governance involves a set of relationships between a company's man-*

---

141   The founders of Applied Corporate Governance™ have developed a different approach to enabling good, ethical and stakeholder-focused governance. The founders are published authors, lecturers and above all practitioners with decades of strategic business experience and the insight to identify the key issues facing all organizations, from the small family business to the public company and from a local charity to a national government. Retrieved from http://www.applied-corporate-governance.com/stakeholder-survey.html

142   The Five Golden Rules view of best corporate governance practice and the holistic approach by which Applied Corporate Governance believes an organization can ensure that a state of good corporate governance exists, or is brought into being if its existence is uncertain. It takes the view that there is an over-riding moral dimension to running a business and that the standard of governance will depend on the moral complexion of the operation. Retrieved from http://www.applied-corporate-governance.com/best-corporate-governance-practice.html#GoldenRules

143   First released in May 1999 and revised in 2004, the OECD Principles are one of the 12 key standards for international financial stability of the Financial Stability Forum (FSF) and form the basis for the corporate governance component of the Report on the Observance of Standards and Codes of the World Bank Group. Retrieved from http://www.oecd.org/document/49/0,3343,en_2649_34813_31530865_1_1_1_1,00.html

*agement, its board, its shareholders and other stakehold-
ers. Corporate governance also provides the structure
through which the objectives of the company are set, and
the means of attaining those objectives and monitoring
performance are determined."*

The methodology of stakeholder analysis can be used to prioritize various stakeholders involved in a project and to determine their accountability mechanism preferences taking into consideration the context and cultural aspects of the project. Accountability is about transparency. If privacy obligations have to be maintained, they have to be maintained with clear criteria about how such obligations are met. And even though financial procedures make up the bulk of accountability framework, reporting on relationships, intent, objectives, methods and impact are all important dimensions to be considered in designing effective accountability mechanisms. Accountability mechanisms record facts and make judgments. They are designed using quantitative and qualitative data, as well as hard and soft, empirical and speculative dimensions. Knowing the rights of an NGO is paramount. Through rights-duty analysis, the specific responsibilities of an NGO are identified and the NGO can account for these responsibilities; and the overall impact of the above combination of people, relationships, money, things, and time have on the rights concerned. Accountability processes must also involve key stakeholders through representative meetings, research, representative assemblies or voting systems. A comprehensive diagnostic report will cover such issues as:

- the people involved,
- lessons learned,
- relationships that emerged,
- quality and standards met,
- money spent, and
- programs money spent.

The Bayer Group's strap line, *"Expertise with Responsibility"* is a fitting description of what NGOs represent. Also, NGO beliefs are so well in line with the Price Waterhouse Cooper's global strap line, '*Together, We Can Change the World*'.

Chapter 7: Appropriate NGO Accountability
Mechanisms

The spirit of accountability is answerability based on the dialectic relationships between the NGO and the society and/or stakeholder groups
of interest (Gray, Bebbington, & Collison, 2006). The spirit of these
relationship requirements is to ensure multi-stakeholder inclusive-
ness. Accountability works with business, government and civil society.
Appropriate accountability tools and processes must not only assure
accountability to donors but also to NGO staff ('internal' accountability)
as well as to the general public and the beneficiaries of NGO services
('downward' accountability). Such internal and downward accountability mechanisms are effective when developed with the local contexts and
the given purposes of the NGO in perspective. Stakeholder participation reinforces transparency and responsiveness by informing people
about, and involving people in, new action taken (Ebrahim, 2003; Slim,
2002).

The community-led HIV/AIDS Initiative in Uganda has proven the
effectiveness of downward and internal accountability mechanisms.
According to the program, the deliverers of public services are accountable primarily to the communities they serve. Superior accountability
has to do with organizational accessibility to societal scrutiny and the
transparency with which affairs are conducted. Transparent NGOs
report on how successful they are meeting their missions and objectives.
Emphasis is placed more on outcomes. Any accountability mechanisms
with emphasis on procedures and compliance with rules and regulations
are short of being productive. OCL tools provide useful mechanisms in
forging relationships among stakeholders. OCL tools offer capabilities
enabling NGOs to be open and responsible for their missions and objectives—what they do and allow involvement of development partners
and facilitate learning and continuous process improvements that lead
to long term social change benefits.

The widespread use and expansion of the World Wide Web has
revolutionized the discovery, access, and retrieval of information. The

Internet has become the doorway to a vast information base and has leveraged the access to information through standard protocols and technologies like Hypertext Markup Language (HTML), active server pages (ASP). Java Server Pages (JSP), web databases and web services. Web services are specific type of software applications using specific IT architecture that are accessible over the World Wide Web through standard communication protocols. A web-based service typically has a web-accessible interface for its clients at the front end and is connected to a database system and other related application suites at the back end. The true success of this technology largely depends on the efficient management of the various components forming the backbone of a web service system.

OCL, defined as "the use of asynchronous computer communication networks to provide social spaces for communities to collaboratively participate in the construction of knowledge" (Bélanger, 2005, p. 3), can be a useful resource for NGOs to maintain accountability relationships with stakeholders. It allows interaction and learning to take place among project stakeholders including beneficiaries of services. Community is a vital part of OCL. Developing and sustaining social interaction is a vital part of any online community. Evidently, an online community is not static, it is made up of people. Therefore, differences in education and technical ability of stakeholder contributions should be considered when developing and sustaining online communities. - is advised. Netiquette literally refers to network etiquette, i.e. the etiquette of cyberspace. And "etiquette" means "the forms required by good breeding or prescribed by authority to be required in social or official life." In other words, netiquette is a set of rules for behaving properly online.

OCL offers the ability for NGOs to be responsive thus improving the efficiency and effectiveness in achieving outcomes. Privacy policies for protecting individually identifiable information in an online or electronic commerce environment will address at least the following elements, with customization and enhancement as appropriate to its own business or industry sector:

- *Adoption and implementation of a privacy policy:* a responsibility an organization engaged in online activities or electronic commerce has to take to foster the adoption and implementation of effective online privacy policies.

- *Notice and disclosure*: providing a clear statement of what privacy mechanism the organization uses, including how to contact the organization, and what steps the organization takes to ensure data quality and access.

- *Choice/consent*: in terms of providing the public with the opportunity to exercise choice regarding how individually identifiable information collected from them online may be used when such use is unrelated to the purpose for which the information was collected.

- *Data security:* taking appropriate measures to assure data reliability and taking reasonable precautions to protect data from loss, misuse or alteration.

- *Data quality and access:* taking reasonable steps to assure data is accurate, complete and timely for the purposes for which it is to be used.

The Online Privacy Alliance[144] is leading and supporting self-regulatory initiatives geared toward creating an environment of trust that fosters the protection of individuals' privacy online and in electronic commerce.

---

144   The Online Privacy Alliance is a cross-industry coalition of more than 80 global companies and associations committed to promoting the privacy of individuals online. Alliance supporters include some of the biggest names in e-commerce, as well as smaller start-up ventures and companies not routinely associated with cyberspace. The group's stated mission is to lead and support self-regulatory initiatives that create an environment of trust and that foster the protection of individuals' privacy online and in electronic commerce. Retrieved from http//:www.alliance.org/

Considerable efforts are being undertaken in various forums, including the Internet Society[145] and the Internet Governance Forum[146] to assess whether existing privacy principles remain relevant and effective. 2010 and 2011 represent important milestones for Privacy: 2010 marks the 30th anniversary of the OECD's Privacy Guidelines. Preparations are also underway for the 30th anniversary, in 2011, of the Council of Europe Convention 108—the first legally binding international privacy instrument. Additionally, in 2009, the International Conference of Data Protection and Privacy Commissioners[147] approved a resolution of

---

145   The Internet Society (ISOC) is a nonprofit organization founded in 1992 to provide leadership in Internet related standards, education, and policy. With offices in Washington D.C., USA, and Geneva, Switzerland, it is dedicated to ensuring the open development, evolution and use of the Internet. The Internet Society provides leadership in addressing issues that confront the future of the Internet, and is the organizational home for the groups responsible for Internet infrastructure standards, including the Internet Engineering Task Force (IETF) and the Internet Architecture Board (IAB). The Internet Society acts not only as a global clearinghouse for Internet information and education but also as a facilitator and coordinator of Internet-related initiatives around the world. For over 15 years ISOC has run international network training programs for developing countries and these have played a vital role in setting up the Internet connections and networks in virtually every country connecting to the Internet during this time. The Internet Society has more than 100 organizational and more than 28,000 individual members in over 80 chapters around the world. Retrieved from http://www.isoc.org/

146   The purpose of the Internet Governance Forum (IGF) is to support the United Nations Secretary-General in carrying out the mandate from the World Summit on the Information Society (WSIS) with regard to convening a new forum for multi-stakeholder policy dialogue - the Internet Governance Forum (IGF). The site provides an interactive, collaborative space where all stakeholders can air their views and exchange ideas. Retrieved from http://www.intgovforum.org/cms/

147   Data protection as a strategy element in the scope of business and international data transfers in a globalized world are core issues at the conference. New advertizing models and new sales techniques are also be discussed, together with their incidence in the field of data protection. Retrieved from http://www.privacyconference2009.org/home/index-iden-idweb.html

international privacy standards. Also, governments around the world are currently developing or adapting their privacy frameworks, while effectively examining the future of privacy in the online environment.

Improvements in technological infrastructure

Any implementation of OCL is dependent upon computer communication networks. Recent improvements and cost-effective OCL technologies and the recent advances in global communications architecture offer unlimited possibilities for OCL technology uses in developing countries. The 'One Laptop Per Child Project' (OLPC)[148], for instance, is an education project through which manufacturers target the mass production of laptops with a price-point suitable for developing countries which has generated much interest in countries OLPC laptops have been deployed which include Uruguay, Peru and Rwanda. In 2002, MIT Professor Nicholas Negroponte[149] experienced first-hand how connected laptops transformed the lives of children and their families in a remote Cambodian village (OLPC, 2009).

Community tele-centers funded primarily by government have also become more common in many developing countries, particularly in rural areas. In the past few years, there has been great interest in

---

148   One Laptop Per Child Project' (OLPC): To create educational opportunities for the world's poorest children by providing each child with a rugged, low-cost, low-power, connected laptop with content and software designed for collaborative, joyful, self-empowered learning. When children have access to this type of tool they get engaged in their own education. They learn, share, create, and collaborate. They become connected to each other, to the world and to a brighter future. Retrieved from http://one.laptop.org/

149   Nicholas Negroponte is a Greek-American architect best known as the founder and Chairman Emeritus of Massachusetts Institute of Technology's Media Lab, and also known as the founder of the One Laptop per Child Association (OLPC). Retrieved from http://en.wikipedia.org/wiki/Nicholas_Negroponte

using tele-centers to provide access to information and communication technologies (ICTs), with projects initiated by governments, the private sector, international donors, and community organizations. Tele-centers have been seen as a means of addressing the lack of ICTs throughout Africa and of assisting in providing universal access, to both telephony and other forms of ICTs.

Further, there is a proliferation of small phone shops in many parts of Africa, run primarily by small entrepreneurs. These centers have started off offering basic telephone services, but many are now moving into fax and even Internet services, as the market develops. Senegal has the largest number of tele-centers supported by the National Telecommunications Company of Senegal (SONATEL): more than 9,000, found on almost every street corner—and increasingly in rural areas—generating a monthly income of approximately USD200 per line, with an estimated contribution of 0.5 percent to the gross domestic product (GDP) of Senegal.

A different private-sector model comes from Africa Online, an Internet company that has set up 261 e-Touch centers in Kenya—mostly in Nairobi. These centers offer e-mail, Internet, fax, photocopying, printing, and telecommunication services. They give users a free e-mail address and charge for usage. Africa Online is also active in Ghana. In 1997 it launched the project 'Email for Everyone', which worked through communication centers—similar to the Senegalese tele-centres or privés. In South Africa, Vodacom has established 1,800 phone shops. These are metal shipping containers with usually 5 to 10 phone lines, costing R24,000 ($3,333) to set up. They are run as franchises and are very profitable. A few are starting to offer fax and even Internet services.

Very different from the aforementioned, micro-projects are the donor-funded tele-centers. The main program has involved a partnership—between the International Telecommunications Union, UNESCO, and the Canadian International Development Research Center (IDRC)—that has established major centers in Mali, Uganda, Mozambique, and South Africa. These centers tend to be much more expensive (up to $250,000) and offer a range of telephony, computing, Internet and information services. The projects stress community participation and sustainability, but to date none have proved that they can be self-sustaining after external funding. Most of these centers are supported by foreign donors, though the national programs for tele-centers in South Africa and Egypt can be included in this category.

Perhaps most well known is the Nakaseke Multipurpose Community Tele-center (MCT) in Uganda. It opened in March 1999 and aims to introduce and test new technologies and applications and to demonstrate the impact of such technologies on development of rural and remote areas. A baseline survey was conducted to establish the nature of information needs of the community and the services. Sixty percent of funding came from international donors, and forty percent from national government. In 2001 a school tax of 59 cents is planned for all 8,000 school children in Nakaseke to subsidize the center.

In Mozambique two pilot tele-centers were established in 1999 in Manhiça and Namaacha (both in Maputo province), funded by the IDRC. They each have four computers, an Internet hub and modem, two printers, backup equipment, a public phone, a fax/phone, an external card-phone, a photocopier, an overhead projector, a whiteboard, a TV with video, a radio and a binder. Current operating costs are just being met by operating income, except the phone bill. Initial conclusions are that long-term economic sustainability depends on the existence of a critical mass of users and the adoption of computer-related services. Over-reliance on phone and photocopy services for income means vulnerability to inevitable future competition and that the major tele-center investment is not justified. Technical support, backup, and continuous staff training are essential, especially for encouraging the developmental and information services, and good communications channels with local authorities and community leaders as well as maximum transparency and information regarding the project are important to success.

In South Africa 63 tele-centers have been established by the Universal Service Agency.[150] Most of these tele-centers are in rural areas.

---

150   The Universal Service and Access Agency of South Africa (UAASA):

Notable also, is the provision of basic telecommunications and informatics services in Transkei region through the introduction of a pilot community tele-centre in Port St. Johns, designed to support multipurpose applications with a large training component covering a wide range of skills training.

In Benin, the International Association of Community Tele-service Centers (CTSC International) on behalf of the Office of P&T, Benin, embarked on the implementation of five pilot community tele-centers in Cotonou, Kraké, Malanville, Parakou and Djougou.

The implementation of a pilot community tele-center in Jakar, the capital of Bumthang district in central Bhutan, where the necessary telecom infrastructure (digital microwave) is already available benefits NGOs who need data-communication and e-mail facilities, and small enterprises (forestry, sawmills, tourist guesthouses, fruits, beekeeping, agriculture, shops, etc.), a hospital and a number of schools).

In Cameroon, the provision of basic telecommunications and informatics services in the Eastern Province of the country through the introduction of three pilot community tele-centers in Garoua Boulai, (some 12,500 inhabitants), Betare Oya and Bertoua (with public call telephone facilities in Belabo and Diang).

In Somalia, the provision of basic telecommunications and informatics services in Galkayo (Mudug) Province through the introduction of a pilot community tele-center, with terminal equipment as above.

The USAASA is established under the Electronic Communications Act No. 36 of 2005, to promote the goals of universal access and universal service in the under serviced areas of South Africa. Under the Electronic Communications Act, the Agency is mandated to: Make recommendations to the Minister of Communications to determine what constitutes universal access by all areas and communities in South Africa; foster adoption and the use of new methods of attaining universal access and service; encourage, facilitate and offer guidance in respect of any scheme to provide universal access and service; encourage any scheme to provide telecommunications services as part of reconstruction and development projects as contemplated in Section 3(a) of the Reconstruction and Development Program Fund Act, 1994 (Act No. 7 of 1994); and Stimulate public awareness of the benefits of telecommunications services.

This would be connected to the national/international network through a small/medium capacity satellite earth station (Arabsat or Intelsat DAMA) with associated wireless access system (cellular radio or MARS) for initially some 10 to 30 individual subscribers and five payphones. A local exchange is also needed.

These small tele-centers have shown there is a greater demand for telephony than had been thought, and a market is growing for ICTs. The larger centers have shown that ICTs can be of use in rural areas as well. Purely market-driven initiatives are likely to increase the digital divide within Africa, and sustaining community access centers needs to be developed. In Pakistan, the establishment and use of multi-purpose community tele-centers, in areas lacking library and telephony facilities has been vital to the social, economic and cultural development of rural and deprived urban communities.

Also, cell phones are becoming quite common in many developing countries. New cell phone technologies, replacing traditional copper wire technology, are proving cheaper and far easier to roll out. OCL can therefore be easily built around cell phone technology. Collaborative applications using telephone technology allowing the sharing of thoughts and impressions in regard to services delivered are highly beneficial to OCL capabilities in developing countries.

However, when developing OCL accountability solutions for NGOs in developing countries, these solutions need to be context specific in terms of each individual location. It is highly unlikely that one solution will meet the needs of a number of varying locations in which NGOs operate. OCL impact on the social fabric of developing countries in terms of alleviating poverty, improving access to health care and education, conserving and fairly distributing resources, and strengthening participation in decision-making processes, cannot be underestimated. Notwithstanding, however, the many opportunities evident with the introduction of technology, social change as a result of technology must be managed carefully, and in line with specific cultural aspects of the community in which NGOs operate. For NGOs that operate in a global context, or for those NGOs that are willing to co-operate and collaborate with colleagues in other countries, OCL can be used in multicultural and global settings to facilitate better understanding among colleagues from different regions of the world because technology can support teams regardless of the locations of individual members (Kirschner, 2004). Recent advances in technology allow sharing on a scale like never before, particularly with the implementation of social networking tools.

Chapter 8: Social Networking Tools

The Internet and the Web are evolving to an environment for collaboration, sharing, innovation and user-created content—the so-called Web 2.0 environment. This environment consists of social and business networks, and it is impacting what people do on the Web and intranets, individually and in communities of practice. The use of Web 2.0 tools and applications is increasing both in small groups inside organizations as well as in social networks—a kind of triad relational model (Technology–People–Community) of social/work life on the Internet. Particularly, social/work groups are becoming sustainable because of the incentives for participants to connect and network with other users. Web 2.0 is by nature immersive, interactive, and collaborative. A discussion of group dynamics that is based on the human needs for trust, support, and sharing, regardless if the setting is a physical or virtual one, follows. The Go2web20[151] has been one of the biggest Web 2.0 directories out there. It is an application built to enable people to stay up to date with all the new services that are born daily into the web. In many cases, Go2web20 has been the first to report the existence of a new application. Today, Go2web20 includes over 3,000 services and more are uploaded everyday. Go2web20 also makes sure to disable services that are no longer working and by doing this Go2web20 ensures a more useful experience when performing a search. This is a natural behavior and logical progress—not all Web 2.0 services live forever, but they serve for as long as they live.

Although social networking tools are often used in open environments where information is freely shared, information can generally be secured for the purposes of OCL for NGOs, and NGOs rely on different uses of social media to meet their brand objectives. Some of the

---

151   Go2web20 was founded in mid-2006, has thousands of unique visitors
      per day, indexes thousands of applications that will help your daily life
      on the net easier, and keep you up to date on the services that you need
      to know about as they arrive on the scene. Retrieved from http://www.
      go2web20.net/

more common social networking implementations include Facebook, MySpace, Twitter, WordPress, Flickr, Foursquare, and Yammer—and there are now literally thousands of such applications.

The 7 Cs of Social Media Usage

There are seven distinct uses of social media in NGOs as business entities[152]. Whatever channel organizations ultimately decide to use to bring their social media idea to life and meet their brand objectives, they are trying to do one of seven things with social media.

- *Communicating*: to many people—communicating typically implies a two-way dialogue. However, the true meaning of communication is all about "conveying information." And that's what most organizations that use social media are doing. They are communicating a message, in other words, broadcasting.

- *Cause support/sponsorship*: helping out a cause such as a patient support society or other non-profit organization is another common use of social media for organizations, and can be a smart approach for NGOs to get as many "*supporters*" as they have. In healthcare, for instance, there are impressive examples of social media tools being skilfully used to get supporters with Merck's

---

152   NGOs, although expected to operate efficiently and effectively and to cover much of their operational costs as possible, do not generate enough funds to enable them meet their day-to-day operational costs. However, it is important to note that a new breed of NGOs called "business NGOs" is now beginning to emerge in Africa. These are NGOs that do combine "business" and development in their mission statements. See also the PDA and UNAIDS Best Practice Collection (2001) on the Strategies to Strengthen NGO Capacity in Resource Mobilization through Business Activities – Retrieved from http://data.unaids.org/Publications/IRC-pub06/jc579-strategies_ngo_en.pdf

program for Gardasil, creating a "semi" unbranded page called '*Take a Step against Cervical Cancer*'[153]. Instead of asking people to be a fan of Gardasil, they ask people to be a fan of fighting cervical cancer.

- *Contests*: there are a number of these types of programs out there and they are common in many industries. The typical idea is to have users submit a video or story about a specific topic, conduct some sort of judging process, and then announce the winners (and award some prizes). Interestingly enough, this category is one of the pharma industry's first forays into social media, back in 2007. Way back then, before every pharma company was on YouTube, Novartis sponsored a contest called Flu Flix. The contest was designed to help raise awareness of the flu and why it's important to get vaccinated. These programs can be great if people actually participate. They participate in two ways. First, actually submitting content to the contest and, second, voting or commenting on other submissions.

- *Program impact research*: nearly everything in social media can be monitored. Through monitoring an NGO can see what people think about program impact. Information gathered while monitoring can be used.

- *Connecting others*: social media networking basically matches people together with those with similar profiles and allows them to share off-site contact information such as email, Skype or telephony applications.

- *Customer service*: while very common in other industries, the NGO community can begin to use some customer service (with both the donors and beneficiaries of

153 "Take a Step against Cervical Cancer" encourages people to join the thousands of people in the fight against cervical cancer and promotes how the simple choices people make can impact their lives and the lives of young females everywhere. Retrieved from http://www.facebook.com/take astepagainstcervicalcancer?v=box_3

program impact being the customers) via social media. Twitter seems to be a popular place for customer service since it also happens to be a place where people tend to complain and need customer service.

- *Community building*: the final way social media is used by NGOs is to create communities. Similar to *"connecting others"* above, this one is about creating a community that is related to NGOs program objectives [Dose of Digital, 2010).

More than 800 million active users log on to Facebook[154] in any given day. The average user has 130 "friends". People spend over 700 billion minutes per month on Facebook. More than one million websites have integrated with Facebook Platform. More than 150 million people engage with Facebook on external websites every month. Two-thirds of comScore's[155] U.S. Top 100 websites and half of comScore's Global Top 100 have integrated with Facebook. Facebook's powerful APIs enable individuals and organizations to create social experiences to drive growth and engagement on their web sites. There

---

154 The Facebook Platform is the set of APIs and tools which enable you to integrate with the social graph to drive registration, personalization, and traffic — whether through applications on Facebook.com or external websites and devices. There are over 900 million objects that people interact with (pages, groups, events and community pages). Average user is connected to 80 community pages, groups and events. Every month, more than 70% of Facebook users engage with Platform applications. Retrieved from http://www.facebook.com/press/info.php?statistics

155 comScore, Inc. (NASDAQ: SCOR) is a global leader in measuring the digital world. This capability is based on a massive, global cross-section of more than 2 million consumers who have given comScore permission to confidentially capture their browsing and transaction behavior, including online and offline purchasing. comScore panelists also participate in survey research that captures and integrates their attitudes and intentions. Through its proprietary technology, comScore measures what matters across a broad spectrum of behavior and attitudes. comScore analysts apply this deep knowledge of customers and competitors to help clients design marketing strategies and tactics. Retrieved from http://www.comscore.com

are a number of Facebook applications now available through cell phone technology, and posts can be made using SMS services. There are a vast variety of add-ons available on Facebook, some of which may be appropriate for OCL by NGOs.

Twitter[156] is a social networking and micro blogging service that allows answers to questions like, *"What are you doing?"* by sending short text messages 140 characters in length, called "tweets", to friends, or "followers." For business, Twitter can be used to broadcast news and blog posts, interact with stakeholders, or to enable easy internal collaboration and group communication. Twitter fundraising has steadily been on the rise in the last two years. Twitter has been used to raise hundreds of thousands of dollars for charities and charitable causes, and has been used to spread awareness about social issues. The power of Twitter is merely a reflection of the power of community. For instance, 12for12k[157] is the combination of social media awareness and fund-raising that aims to change the lives of millions worldwide, by using the power and outreach of social media to spread the word. From Twitter to Facebook, blogs to social media newsrooms and more, 12for12k is helping supported charities connect with as wide an audience as possible.

---

156   Twitter has many uses for both personal and business use. It's a great way to keep in touch with friends and quickly broadcast information. People use Twitter to ask questions, follow people that are interesting, promote links to various websites, share news stories. Retrieved from http://tweeternet.com/#usefulness

157   12for12k uses social media-led outreach to raise funds for qualified charitable organizations. To ensure as much help continues to go to those who need it the most, all the partners in 12for12k are offering their time and services for free. Retrieved from http://12for12k.org/

The fundraising initiatives—Twestival[158], Kickstarter[159] and Indiegogo[160]—are primary examples of crowdfunding applications effectively harnessing the power of social media to raise money at both global and local levels.

The relationships among supporters and those in need that come about as a result of social media fundraising can and should continue to grow after a charity event. People like to see where their money is going and whom it's affecting. This gives them incentive to come back next year and continue to give. To connect the Tweetsgiving community directly to the people the campaign is impacting is a critical way of direct communication with stakeholders. With online tools, there is no reason stakeholders and beneficiaries all cannot be kept abreast. The Twitterkids of Tanzania[161] and their participation with their parents and teachers in TweetsGiving are just one example of how that's possible.

If several different networking tools are warranted because of their unique features there are now user interfaces such as TweetDeck[162] that allow the same information to be entered once and posted to a number of different social networking tools including Twitter and Facebook. TweetDeck offers personal browsers for staying in touch with what's happening now, connecting with contacts across Twitter, Facebook, MySpace, LinkedIn and more. With TweetDeck anyone can tweet like

---

158   Twestival™ (or Twitter Festival) is a global movement which uses the power of social media to organize offline events that mobilize communities in support of local causes. Retrieved from http://www.twestival.com/

159   Kickstarter is an American-based private for-profit company founded in 2009 that provides through its website tools to fund raise for creative projects via crowd funding. Retrieved from http://www.kickstarter.com/

160   *Indiegogo* is an international crowd funding site where anyone can raise money for film, music, art, charity, small businesses, gaming, theater, and more. Retrieved from http://www.indiegogo.com/

161   Twitter Kids of Tanzania is the Epic Change Blog that amplifies the voices and impact of grassroots change makers and social entrepreneurs. Retrieved from http://epicchange.org/

162   TweetDeck enables users to connect with Facebook and MySpace friends directly by updating status, posting photos or videos, commenting, liking and grouping friends to make it easier to follow. Retrieved from http://www.tweetdeck.com/

a pro; can, for instance, customize Twitter experience with columns, groups, saved searches and automatic updates helping people to effortlessly stay updated with the people and topics they care about.

The iPad[163] is a breakthrough platform for magazines, allowing publishers to do more than they ever could before. The iPad is a mobile computing device, which has been described by some as a cross between the iPhone and a MacBook laptop.

There are plenty of RSS and Web Readers that are resources NGOs can use, and instead of trying to list them all, a handful are listed in this book, including links to other sites that list even more. For web-based readers, some web sites let you read all your feed subscription in one place, and are handy if you read these from different locations, such as home and work. For example:

- NewsGator[164]: NewsGator's Social Networking solutions help people overcome business challenges by providing an integrated, behind-the-firewall, social computing platform that supports collaboration, facilitates communication, and improves worker knowledge.

- Delicious[165] is a social bookmarking service, which means you can save all your bookmarks online, share them with other people, and see what other people are bookmarking.

---

163 iPad launched, the magazine's publisher, Bonnier, introduced Popular Science+, an iPad app that delivers everything readers love about the print magazine - great storytelling, pacing, and images — in an immersive experience that takes full advantage of the Multi-Touch features of iPad. The convergence of great content and new technology helped make Popular Science+ one of the best-reviewed and most downloaded iPad apps. Retrieved from http://www.apple.com/ipad/apps-for-ipad/popular-science/

164 NewsGator offers a series of unique services that guides users down the Enterprise 2.0 path to arrive at solutions perfectly tailored to their needs. Retrieved from http://www.newsgator.com/

165 Delicious shows users the most popular bookmarks being saved right across many areas of interest. In addition, its search and tagging tools help users of Delicious keep track of their entire bookmark collection and find tasty new bookmarks from various people. Retrieved from http://www.delicious.com/

- Mobile Refdesk[166] is available on all carriers from any mobile Internet enabled device through its universal resource locator. Mobile Refdesk and the Internet Public Library[167] contains links to a list of newspapers all over the world and links to their websites, although the format and display may be different due to the small screen available on the mobile device.

- Google News[168] is a free news aggregator provided and operated by Google, Inc., selecting most up-to-date information from thousands of publications by an automatic aggregation algorithm.

- Yahoo! News[169] is a similar news aggregator provided and operated by Yahoo!

---

166   Mobile Refdesk is available on all carriers from any mobile Internet enabled device. Mobile Refdesk contains links to the most popular sites on the regular Refdesk homepage, although the format and display may be different due to the small screen available on the mobile device. Retrieved from http://m.refdesk.com

167   ipl2 is the result of a merger of the Internet Public Library (IPL) and the Librarians' Internet Index (LII). Retrieved from http://www.ipl.org/div/news/

168   Google News is a computer-generated news site that aggregates headlines from news sources worldwide, groups similar stories together and displays them according to each reader's personalized interests. Google News offers links to several articles on every story, so readers can first decide what subject interests them and then select which publishers' accounts of each story they would like to read. Articles are selected and ranked by computers that evaluate, among other things, how often and on what sites a story appears online. Google News also ranks based on certain characteristics of news content such as freshness, location, relevance and diversity. As a result, stories are sorted without regard to political viewpoint or ideology and readers can choose from a wide variety of perspectives on any given story. Retrieved from http://news.google.com/

169   Yahoo! News is an Internet-based news aggregator by Yahoo!. It categorizes news into "Top Stories", "U.S. National", "World", "Business", "Entertainment", "Science", "Health", "Weather", "Most Popular", "News Photos", "Op/Ed", and "Local News". Articles in Yahoo! News come from news services, such as Associated Press, Reuters, Agence France-Presse, Fox

- NGO Portal[170] is an online resource that provides information related to all aspects of NGOs.
- NGO Monitor[171] provides information and analysis, promotes accountability, and supports discussion on the reports and activities of NGOs (non-governmental organizations) claiming to advance human rights and humanitarian agendas.
- *Monthly Developments Magazine*[172] provides in-depth news and commentary on global trends that affect relief, refugee and development work.
- NGO News[173] is a great source of information about all kinds of NGO activities related news and information worldwide.

There are also e-tools of engagement—email services—almost all NGOs can use to communicate more quickly at lower cost, to recruit new members and to solicit financial support, to disseminate informa-

---

News, ABC News, NPR, USA Today, CNN.com, CBC News, Seven News, and BBC News. Retrieved from http://news.yahoo.com/

170   NGO Portal is a resource for NGOs covering broad areas of NGOs including NGO database, database of training Institutes, NGO financial management, NGO human resources and administration management, NGO grants, NGO development jobs, funding agencies database, NGI legal aspects, NGO project management, NGO news. Retrieved from http://www.ngoportal.org/

171   NGO Monitor generates and distributes critical analysis and reports on the output of the international NGO community for the benefit of government policy makers, journalists, philanthropic organizations and the general public. Retrieved from http://www.ngo-monitor.org/index.php/

172   *Monthly Developments Magazine* features the latest information on the work of NGOs around the world and keeps readers up to date on legislative action in Congress that could impact U.S. foreign assistance to developing countries. *Monthly Developments Magazine* also describes new resources for relief and development workers, professional growth opportunities, upcoming events and international employment opportunities. Retrieved from http://www.monthlydevelopments.org/

173   NGO News has a vast collection of NGO related information and links. Retrieved from http://ngonewsbd.com/

tional resources to governments and the public, and to realize innovative ideas. These email services offer plenty of storage, effective spam filtering, a fast interface, desktop email program and mobile access, and more. Some of the popular email services include the following:

- *Gmail*[174]: Gmail is the Google approach to email, chat and social networking. Practically unlimited free online storage allows you to collect all your messages, and Gmail's simple but very smart interface lets you find mail precisely and see it in context without effort. POP and powerful IMAP access bring Gmail to any email program or device. Gmail puts contextual advertising next to the emails you read.

- *GMX Mail—Free E-Mail*[175]: GMX Mail offers free GMX e-mail address.

- *FAXCOM Anywhere*[176]: Get an internet fax number that sends and receives faxes online.

---

174   Gmail is a free, advertising-supported email service provided by Google. Users may access Gmail as secure webmail, as well as via POP3 or IMAP4 protocols. Retrieved from https://mail.google.com/
175   GMX Mail is a free webmail service provided by GMX (Global Mail eXchange, in Germany: Global Message eXchange). Founded in 1997, GMX is a subsidiary of United Internet AG, a stock-listed company in Germany, and a sister company to 1&1 Internet and Fasthosts Internet. In addition to an e-mail address, each GMX account includes a Mail Collector, Address Book, Organizer, and File Storage. One user can register up to 10 individual GMX e-mail addresses. Retrieved from http://www.gmx.com/
176   FAXCOM *Anywhere* is for the organization that wants to utilize a fax server without incurring the costs of implementing and maintaining a fax server on site. Users send and receive faxes from their desktop computer— via a secure Internet connection to a virtual fax server at Biscom's hosted facility. As your fax needs grow, FAXCOM *Anywhere* provides a growth path to FAXCOM Server as a premise solution. Retrieved from http://www.faxcomanywhere.com/

- *AIM Mail—Free Email Service*[177]: AIM Mail, AOL's free web-based email service, with unlimited online storage, spam protection and easy to use interface.

- *Yahoo! Mail—Free Email Service*[178]: Yahoo! Mail is an email program on the web and mobile devices with unlimited storage, SMS texting and instant messaging.

- *Inbox.com*[179] offers free 5 GB of online mailbox space as well as POP access with a fast web interface which includes rich text editing, threading and free-form labels as well as solid spam and virus filtering.

- *FastMail*[180] is a free email service with IMAP access, useful features, and web interface.

- *Windows Live Hotmail*[181] is the world's second largest web-based email service after Gmail; available in 36 different languages.

---

177   AOL Mail is a free web-based email (webmail) service provided by AOL. The service is sometimes referred to as AIM Mail where AIM stands for AOL Instant Messenger which is AOL's instant messaging service. Retrieved from http://www.aim.com/

178   Yahoo! Mail is a free e-mail service offered by the American search engine company Yahoo! Retrieved from https://login.yahoo.com/

179   Inbox.com offers free user-friendly webmail with advanced functions, spam protection and more. Inbox offers a highly polished, fast and functional way to access it via either the web (including speedy search, free-form labels and reading mail by conversation) or through POP in your email program. Retrieved from http://www.inbox.com/

180   FastMail.FM is an email provider, offering email addresses and storage space for incoming emails in the same way Hotmail, GMail and Yahoo!Mail do. Users can manage email from any computer connected to the internet with a web-browser. Retrieved from https://www.fastmail.fm/

181   Hotmail (officially Microsoft Hotmail, previously Windows Live Hotmail and MSN Hotmail) is a free web-based email service operated by Microsoft as part of Windows Live. One of the first web-based email services, it was founded by Sabeer Bhatia and Jack Smith and launched in July 1996 as "HoTMaiL". It was acquired by Microsoft in 1997 for an estimated $400 million, and shortly after, it was rebranded as "MSN Hotmail". The current version was released in 2011. Hotmail features unlimited storage, Ajax, and integration with Microsoft's instant messaging (Windows

Other useful resources include the following:

- *Email Finder*[182]: Using just someone's name, users can utilize Email Finder's proprietary directory and search methods to quickly scour a variety of phone book sources, public records, and other databases online for his or her email address. In addition to an email address search based on someone's name, Email Finder can also find a person's address as well as other related details.

- *QuODA*[183] is an assessment of the Quality of Official Development Assistance (ODA) provided by 23 donor countries and more than 150 aid agencies. Aid quality is assessed using 30 indicators grouped in four dimensions that reflect the international consensus of what constitutes high-quality aid, i.e. *Maximizing Efficiency, Fostering Institutions, Reducing Burden, Transparency and Learning.*

- *Africa Rural Connect*[184]: Africa Rural Connect blends the inside knowledge of Africans, Peace Corps Volunteers, and African scholars.

Live Messenger), calendar (Hotmail Calendar),file hosting service (Sky-Drive), and contacts platform. Retrieved from http://www.hotmail.com/

182   Email Finder offers innovative service to reconnect with old friends from high school, find a long lost relative, or verify contact information you have in your e-mail address book. It's fast, easy, and free to run your initial search. Retrieved from http://www.emailfinder.com/

183   Rankings can be viewed in separate indices and in the Quality of Aid Diamond, which makes it possible to quickly compare countries and agencies across all four dimensions. The authors hope that QuODA will be a catalyst for lively debates and, more importantly, for substantial improvements in how aid is provided.

184   Africa Rural Connect (ARC), a program of the National Peace Corps Association, is an online global collaboration network where knowledgeable people work together to communicate and respond to the needs of African farmers. The ARC platform allows you take an active role in building development initiatives that can directly affect the lives of rural farmers. Retrieved from http://arc.peacecorpsconnect.org/

- *The Humanitarian Innovations Fund [HIF]*[185] has been
  created through a new partnership between ALNAP
  and ELRHA[186] in a joint effort to significantly enhance
  the contribution of innovation to improving humanitarian performance in operational settings. The purpose
  of the Humanitarian Innovations Fund will be to support the identification, development, testing and dissemination of new technologies and processes that will
  lead to demonstrated and cost-effective improvements
  in humanitarian outcomes. The Fund, which is being
  launched with a generous start-up investment from the
  UK Government's Department for International Development, aims to attract further investment from a range
  of donors that seek to support efforts to improve the
  quality and effectiveness of humanitarian programs.

---

185   The Humanitarian Innovation Fund (HIF) will support organizations working in countries struck by humanitarian crises such as Haiti or
Pakistan to develop, test and share new technologies and processes that
will contribute to more effective and cost-efficient humanitarian aid in the
future. Created through a partnership between two leading initiatives in
the humanitarian sector, ELRHA and ALNAP, with a £900,000 start up investment from the UK Department for International Development (DFID),
this fund represents a collective effort to enhance the contribution of innovation to improving humanitarian performance in the field. The fund will
be hosted by Save the Children UK as part of their ongoing support to the
ELRHA initiative. Retrieved from http://www.alnap.org/initiatives/current/
innovations/fund.aspx

186   LRHA is committed to stimulating and supporting research partnerships that are focused on the current and future challenges of the
humanitarian sector. In consultation with some of the largest and most
active humanitarian agencies we have identified four thematic areas where
research partnerships with Higher Education are needed: collaborative
working, innovation and future preparedness, humanitarian principles and
operational challenges. Retrieved from http://www.elrha.org/

Chapter 9: OCL Implementation Contextual Issues

The use of OCL for accountability purposes is an evolving phenomenon for NGOs in developing countries. A conceptual framework of OCL technology for helping NGOs implement accountability mechanisms in their project delivery strategy is necessary. In the context of this subject, NGOs' project accountability strategy is defined as the set of project accountability methods that are adopted for sharing organizational objectives. The implementation framework is based upon observations of actual use of OCL technology and upon concepts developed within the academic disciplines of applied management and decision sciences studying organizational management. The proposed framework includes an inventory of actions needed (1) to implement accountability mechanisms, (2) to build knowledge on the introduced approaches, and (3) to assess the outcome of OCL implementation. Finally, recommendations are provided to practitioners who are responsible for managing the OCL delivery processes at several levels, including planning, procurement, and project management.

Definition of desired outcomes: Desired organizational outcomes are different to objectives, outputs, and deliverables in that they:

o   are defined according to neuroscience rules (to increase resonance with all parties);

o   describe a future organization state (what success looks like);

o   are measurable (by a true/false question).

Desired organizational outcomes describe what the organization really wants, where it wants to be at the end of the project. This is often quite different to where it initially says it wants to be. So many of the problems on projects with "unrealistic expectations", changing requirements, dissatisfaction with project outcomes and alike stem from the lack of clarity about what the organization's desired outcomes really are. Once the outcomes are known and agreed all aspects of the project can be focused on their delivery. And, as the realization of the program benefits are based on the delivery of the outcomes, this increased focus on the outcomes automatically increases the value realized.

Identification of stakeholders (stakeholder analysis)

Effective strategies for stakeholder participation must be based on good analysis of individuals, groups, and institutions with an interest in a project. Stakeholder analysis is advisable for all projects. Participatory approaches are important for a sustainable and effective NGO program. Identification of key stakeholders through stakeholder analysis and listing key issues for partnership with stakeholders is critical to the success of any NGO. The series of steps involved in negotiating participation of other stakeholders in NGO activities and the extent to which participation is feasible, sensible and cost effective can be explored in relation to the type of aid and sector.

Stakeholder analysis is the identification of a project's key stakeholders, an assessment of their interests, and the ways in which these interests affect project riskiness and viability. It is linked to both institutional appraisal and social analysis: drawing on the information deriving from these approaches, but also contributing to the combining of such data in a single framework.

Stakeholders are persons, groups or institutions with interests in a project or program. Primary stakeholders are those ultimately affected, either positively (beneficiaries) or negatively (for example, those involuntarily resettled). Secondary stakeholders are the intermediaries in the aid delivery process. This definition of stakeholders includes both winners and losers, and those involved or excluded from decision-making processes. Key stakeholders are those who can significantly influence, or are important to the success of the project.

Stakeholder analysis helps administrators and advisors to assess a project environment. More specifically, doing a stakeholder analysis can:

- draw out the interests of stakeholders in relation to the problems which the project is seeking to address (at the identification stage) or the purpose of the project (once it has started).
- identify conflicts of interests between stakeholders, which will influence assessment of a project's riskiness before funds are committed (which is particularly important for process projects).
- help to identify relations between stakeholders which can be built upon, and may enable "coalitions" of project sponsorship, ownership and cooperation.
- help to assess the appropriate type of participation by different stakeholders, at successive stages of the project cycle.

There are several steps to doing a stakeholder analysis:

- draw up a "stakeholder table";
- do an assessment of each stakeholder's importance to project success and their relative power/influence;
- identify risks and assumptions which will affect project design and success.

Identification and adaptation of technology solutions to enable collaboration

A considerable amount of progress has to be made in building technical capacity at the individual and institutional levels, vulnerability assessment, adaptation planning, the development of the tools and methodologies, and policy formulation. There is a need to prepare all project stakeholders, including clients and beneficiaries, for the imminent implementation of technology adaptation plans and policies.

The participatory planning process from which NGO accountability programs are developed have to involve stakeholders in defining the priorities, objectives, rules and structures of the project, and the implementation process, and the subsequent organizational structures that fostered and facilitated stakeholder involvement in management and implementation of the project, and the formulation of resulting policies.

To ensure effective adaptation the participatory process must be extended to all stakeholders that will be involved in the adaptation process. The steps in a participatory process are similar to conventional approaches to planning, and include problem identification, definition of goals and objectives, collection and analysis of information, identification of options, formulation of plans and decisions, implementation, and monitoring and evaluation:

- *Gather and analyze all relevant information*: Find and analyze information from diverse sources. Use such relevant information to form opinions, make decisions, and take action. Establish criteria for the quality and appropriateness of the information. Assess the value of the information. Use the information to make informed decisions.

- To formulate an effective accountability strategy, it's essential to understand two basic questions: What do you want to be accountable for; and what are the most common accountability mechanisms that have worked for other organizations? Information gathering and analysis is a field of strategic research that specializes in the collection and analysis of information about effective OCL technology. Information gathering and analysis is about adhering to a strict ethical code by collecting bits of information that are available either in the public domain or from other players in the marketplace. The goal is to amass enough data to make meaningful comparisons about accountability mechanisms that work—and to make better-informed strategic decisions as a result. Here's how to get started.

o   *A focused goal:* define what you want to be accountable for and develop a specific accountability "assignment."

o   *Unwavering ethics:* it's tempting to cut corners or resort to dubious techniques when hunting for proprietary information. Don't do it.

o   *Research tools:* online databases on emerging OCL technology are an essential place to begin research, although many require a subscription. (Some OCL technological innovations have been discussed in this book.)

o   *Resourcefulness:* competitive information is seldom served up on a silver platter. Finding the information needed will inevitably require creativity and adaptability.

Apply learning to the organization to improve outcomes

The transfer of knowledge as a social activity has created opportunities for workers to learn as they work, by connecting with someone with the answers, who may live anywhere in the world. In 1966, Peter Drucker coined the term the '*knowledge worker.*' While manual workers use their hands to produce goods or services, 'knowledge workers' use their heads to produce ideas, knowledge, and information. While Web 1.0 succeeded in connecting workers across the globe, most of the content was static and top-down. Web 2.0 technologies, known as SLATES (search, links, authoring, tags, extensions, and signals) have given a new energy to social learning, by making it easier to access information, which is immediate, relevant and personalized to individual learning needs.

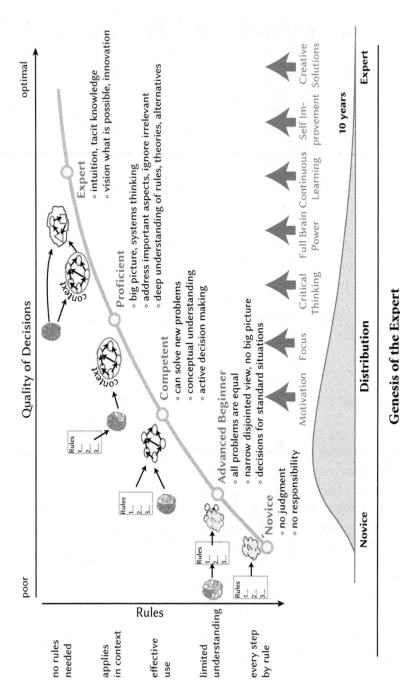

Genesis of the Expert

Graphics based on http://softwarecreation.org/images/2009/novice-expert.jpg. Andriy Solovey, April 6, 2009.

For professionals learning at the workplace, social learning tools have become very useful and manageable. Social learning—and its associated tools—can help achieve business goals. Social learning, or sharing knowledge, has the following affect on business outcomes—(1) productive employees, (2) speed of business, flexibility, and quality; and (3) innovation—all of which are required for business success.

In the *Dreyfus Model* of skill acquisition, there are five stages in the process, Novice, Beginner, Competent, Expert, and Proficient.

Social learning plays a critical role in helping employees acquire the knowledge they need to become productive (outcome 1) as well as affecting the success of a business (outcomes 2 and 3). Organizations can use social media tools to supplement formal learning. These tools enable reflection and practice during and after formal learning. Learners can use tools such as Facebook, microblogging[187] (e.g. Twitter or Yammer[188]), and Google+[189] before, during, and after formal learning experiences. Jane Harts Center for Performance Management[190] pro-

---

187   Microblogging.com is a site covering the latest news from the social media and microblogging world. The site features news, reviews, and a directory of microblogging sites and applications. Retrieved from http://microblogging.com/

188   Yammer is revolutionizing internal corporate communications by bringing together all of a company's employees inside a private and secure enterprise social network. Although Yammer is as easy to use as consumer products like Facebook or Twitter, its enterprise-grade software is built from the ground up to drive business objectives. Yammer enables users to communicate, collaborate, and share more easily and efficiently than ever before. It reduces the need for meetings, increases communication across silos, surfaces pockets of expertise and connects remote workers. Retrieved from https://www.yammer.com/

189   Google+, a social network operated by Google, Inc., launched on June 28th, 2011 with integrations across a number of Google products, including Buzz and Profiles. One key element of Google+ is a focus on targeted sharing within subsets of your social group, which are what Google calls Circles. Circles are simply small groups of people that you can share to, each with names like friends, family, classmates and co-workers. Retrieved from https://plus.google.com/

190   The Jane Harts Center for Performance Management provides independent advice and consultancy on the use of technologies for learning

vides some excellent tips. Self-directed learning is easier with social media. Learners can use Twitter, Linkedin and Facebook to discuss topics, ask questions and network. There are also online classes, blogs, and podcasts developed by experts.

Social learning facilitates quality, efficiency, and speed which are all excellent outcomes for business success. Social learning has always made a solid contribution, but the process was informal, localized, non-searchable, and slow. Some learning occurred during large company meetings, or team-based activities, which generally ended with the project. Social learning also occurred when competent workers who shared common work practices formed communities of practice around common work practices, aims or interests, like those days when trade guilds were the norm.

Leading organizations, such as Intel[191], IBM[192], Qualcomm[193], and Accenture[194] are effectively using Enterprise 2.0 solutions to generate

---

and performance. The website hosts a number of major resources, including a Directory of Learning & Performance Tools that contains over 2,000 tools. Retrieved from http://c4lpt.co.uk/

191   By partnering with governments and organizations, Intel is making technology more accessible around the world by making PCs more affordable through innovative PC purchase programs. Retrieved from http://www.intel.com/

192   With over 175,000 professionals, IBM is the largest services provider in the world. With specialties such as analytics, IBM helps clients make their systems smarter. Retrieved from http://www.ibm.com/ibm/ideas-fromibm/us/library/index6.shtml

193   Qualcomm's technology connects organizations wherever they are in the world. Qualcomm manufactures chipsets, license technology, and provide communication services around the world. In a global economy, Qualcomm is the link to markets and opportunity. Retrieved from http://www.qualcomm.com/

194   Accenture turns adversity to advantage. A corporation with high performers turning periods of uncertainty to their advantage by fully integrating a risk-management program, which serves not only as a defensive tactic but also as an offensive weapon. Accenture identifies steps that can help its clients use risk management for competitive advantage. Retrieved from www.accenture.com

social networking platforms, complete with wikis, blogging, microblogging, online profiles, and online communities.

The only way to achieve competitive advantage is to treat knowledge as a corporate asset. "Unlike material assets, which decrease as they are used, ideas breed ideas and shared knowledge stays with the giver while it enriches the receiver (Davenport and Prusak, *Working Knowledge*, 1998). For example, IBM has taken this idea seriously with its crowd-sourcing jams, which has identified 10 best incubator businesses, which IBM funded with USD100 million. Social networking thus enables employees from all levels, novice to proficient, to innovate. Using microblogging, wikis, blogs, and tools like Facebook, employees can brainstorm ways to identify new products, improve processes and increase time to promote programs and services.

Shared learning among NGOs to tackle National and International Issues

Current economic, social and political trends are affecting the NGO world, and there are implications for policy and practice. The interconnected themes are of globalization, inequality and insecurity; the reform of international co-operation as foreign aid declines; and the dilemmas of humanitarian action in complex political emergencies, play a visible role in all of these. NGO roles, relationships, capacities and accountabilities, therefore, have to change for NGOs to be successful. Globalization generates shifting patterns of poverty and insecurity both within and between countries that call for new and international responses. As actors in an emerging global civil society, NGOs can help to create a countervailing force to the processes that exploit and exclude people by re-distributing assets and opportunities, injecting social values into market processes, and holding economic institutions to account for their actions. This represents the cutting edge of much NGO work today.

As foreign aid declines, new forms of international co-operation are emerging to meet the realities of this changing world, with a focus on rules and standards rather than subsidized resource transfers. In this context, the key question is whether the regimes of the future will benefit poor people and poor countries. NGOs have an important role to play in ensuring that the poor benefit—by building strong domestic constituencies for international co-operation, forging transnational alliances that represent poor peoples' interests in more pluralistic structures of governance, and enhancing the capacity of civic groups to participate at every level.

Intra-state conflict is characteristic of the post-Cold War disorder and the insecurity that global inequalities breed. Caught between the scale of human suffering and the international community's unwillingness to tackle the politics of humanitarian intervention, NGOs have been drawn more deeply into a tangled web of tensions and dilemmas. This has led to an unprecedented period of self-examination, and a radical re-assessment of NGO roles in the humanitarian arena. A traditional relief focus has given way to a range of inter-connected peace-building, conflict-resolution, advocacy and humanitarian assistance strategies that try to lever macro-level changes as well as positive results on the ground.

Underlying these three trends is the need for new forms of solidarity—or new "social contracts"—between citizens and authorities at different levels of the world system. It is these new relationships—expressed through partnerships, alliances and other forms of co-operation—that provide the framework for NGO innovations, but they also require major changes in NGOs as organizations: a move from "development-as-delivery" to "development-as-leverage"; new relationships with corporations, elements of states, the military, international institutions and other groups in civil society; and different capacities to mediate these links. When relationships and interests become more complex and diffuse, clear accountability procedures are paramount. If they are not to be marginalized as components of a global welfare state, NGOs must demonstrate that they have the right to be treated as major actors in emerging international civil society.

Today, NGOs share in the same mixture of feelings that permeates the wider field of politics, ideas and social activism. There is plenty of excitement about new possibilities, tempered by widespread anxiety about the future. In the NGO world, this feeling of excitement stems from the opportunities for civic action that global trends are creating, on a scale never witnessed before; the anxiety arises because more critical questions are being asked about the role development NGOs will play in occupying aid-dependent intermediaries, especially aid-dependent intermediaries that lack any democratic means of governance and accountability. It is essential, therefore, to generate a broader framework that relates changes inside the NGO community to the great economic and political questions of these times than currently exists, so helping the NGO community to respond more effectively to global trends to the benefit of those they seek to serve.

The roles of NGOs have to be redefined in terms of re-shaping the processes of an evolving global capitalism so that peoples can enjoy the fruits of economic progress without losing what gives meaning to their lives. Globalization as technology-driven in terms of electronic communication, declining transport costs, more flexible forms of economic organization, and the growing importance of mobile assets (like finance and knowledge) establish an increasingly uniform horizon of production possibilities across national borders, integrating markets around the world and internationalizing decisions about jobs and investment. The consequences of this process in a world of unequal producers and consumers are well-known—spectacular rewards for those well-endowed with the conditions required to take advantage of these opportunities; increasing pressures on those less well-endowed to sell their labor, family life or environment cheaply in order to make a living; and rising inequality between these two groups, both within and between countries.

The existing patterns of global poverty with their levels of inequality in the world and the need for reform of international cooperation call for new forms of solidarity or new "social contracts" between citizens and new structures of authority. It is these new relationships—expressed through partnerships, alliances and other forms of collaboration—that provide the framework for NGO innovations in economics, politics and social policy. NGOs are therefore obliged to develop different roles, relationships and capacities. In that sense, the over-arching role of NGOs is to "help revision the world as an ever-growing web of non-exploitative relationships" (Fowler 1997). Translating these principles into practice at different levels of the world economy is difficult and complex, but the case for doing so is clear. Despite the disagreements and probable future fragmentation of NGOs in both North and South, all agree that there are increasing opportunities to work together across institutional boundaries in order to influence the forces that underpin poverty and discrimination, finding partnerships and synergies where few existed before, and molding not just a strong civil society but a society that is just and civil in all that it does. NGOs continue their role as carers of last resort, operating safety-nets, and providing welfare to the casualties of globalization, especially in countries where the transition from protected markets has been far too rapid (as in the former Soviet Union).

At the global level, successful strategies must be connected to supportive actions in other parts of the international system. Globalization means, not only that NGOs must engage more strategically with market forces on a much bigger scale than before, but do so in ways which link micro- to macro-forces together in a coherent way. In the same vein, NGOs are becoming more strategic in their lobbying of the International Financial Institutions, the monitoring of international commitments (like Social Watch[195]), and the democratization of global economic and other regimes (like the World Trade Organization and the proposed Multilateral Agreement on Investment).

Underlying all these strategies is the need for NGOs to put their own house in order by reducing dysfunctional competition in relief funding and operations; working more closely with Southern groups to build up their relief and peace-building capacity, and widen the current Northern-centric humanitarian policy dialogue; making a reality of codes of

---

195   Social Watch, an international network of non-governmental organizations that monitors how far governments are fulfilling their commitments to end poverty and gender discrimination. Retrieved from http://www.socialwatch.org/

conduct by institutionalizing accountability, including to beneficiaries; and developing 'peace audits' to evaluate the impact of their activities on the processes that lead to conflict (Goodhand and Hulme 1998b).

Clearly, NGOs operate in so many contexts and at so many levels that generalization is hazardous. However, some trends can be identified in relation to the need to think and act globally. It is difficult to see how NGOs could re-shape the costs and benefits of global change through stand-alone projects at the local level, funding, or the delivery of basic social and economic services. Instead they must build outwards from concrete innovations at grassroots level to connect with the forces that influence patterns of poverty, prejudice and violence: exclusionary economics, discriminatory politics, selfish and violent personal behavior, and the capture of the world of knowledge and ideas by elites. In a sense this is what NGOs are already doing, by integrating micro- and macro-level action in their project and advocacy activities, but the changing global context challenges them to make this their natural way of working instead of something bolted on to mainstream activities as an optional extra. Moving from development as delivery to development as leverage is the fundamental change that characterizes this shift, and it has major implications for the ways in which NGOs organize themselves, raise and spend their resources, and relate to others.

In future, NGOs will need to find better ways of building constituencies for their work at every level; methods of working together through strategic partnerships that link local and global processes together; and a much more effective method of identifying barriers to change and points of leverage where their combined experience gives them authority and voice. By sinking roots into their own societies and making connections with others inside and outside civil society, NGOs can generate more potential to influence things where it really matters because of the multiplier effects that come from activating a concerned citizenry to work for change in a wider range of settings.

The new global agenda requires, not only that NGOs link with each-other in different ways, but also that they forge relationships with other groups in civil society which can reach further and deeper into the mainstream of politics and economics—like trade unions, consumer groups, the women's and environmental movements, universities and think-tanks, and the news media—eventually creating a global movement for sustainable development. New ways of talking and relating to different sections of the public are needed, especially relating to young men and women; and the essential need to loosen or manage the relationship between NGOs and official donors so that the "piper(s) do not call an inappropriate tune" for organizations that claim to respond to the voices of the people they serve.

The whole purpose of OCL for NGOs is to develop organizational learning relevant to the outcomes of the principal purposes or missions of NGOs. It is therefore necessary to define mission specific outcomes and to identify all participating stakeholders in the OCL process to determine and implement OCL technology solutions and worthwhile social networking tools to allow online collaboration among stakeholders. OCL processes should be shared positive experiences, allowing identification of opportunities to improve levels of services, leading to better outcomes, and promoting collaborative learning partnerships among NGOs are encouraged.

Chapter 10: Research Directions

Suggested research directions reflect on a framework for implementation of OCL as a means of fulfilling accountability obligations and achieving social change in a manner which has been rarely used before. There is a wealth of research opportunities which could be investigated. One obvious direction is to undertake an action research project on NGOs implementing the OCL framework. Other research opportunities include comparison between NGOs in developed and developing countries to see where the similarities and differences lie, and whether the accountability obligations are significantly different in both scenarios. Greater research into the technologies used in developing countries and the spread of mobile telephony is also a research opportunity which should prove to be of benefit to NGOs operating in those countries.

Also various methods of extending the rollout of ICTs in developing countries need to be considered and these require different kinds of research and support. Efforts should go toward models that can be reproduced, while acknowledging that there are different ways this can happen. Straight commercial involvement with companies like Africa Online and others moving into this market if ICTs prove to be lucrative in developing countries is a possibility. As well, subsidized long-term international funding may not be sustainable, but there is a case for local public funding for some projects, as with schools, clinics, and—in some countries—libraries. However, rarely should the funding be 100 percent (all the economic lessons of entrepreneurship should be used). However, this route is uncertain because most African governments have very tight finances, and in many areas the state is tending to withdraw funding for major public projects including education, health, and public libraries. Stepping up migration is another possibility. Perhaps the way with the greatest potential to bring access to ICTs throughout Africa is to support smaller businesses and community organizations that develop new services themselves. If they are offering telephony, they can be the support required to offer mobile and Internet services.

Paramount among things that could facilitate the rollout of ICTs in developing countries include availability of:

- economic return information to persuade investment;
- evidence of wider social impact sufficient to encourage public funding; and
- experiential knowledge on how local risks could be managed making migration easier.

These three are not exclusive categories; a range of external commercial funding, public funding, and smaller entrepreneurial activity can work together. In particular, there is less work on stepping up migration. Support through guides for the thousands of micro-entrepreneurs tells about why and how to offer fax, messaging, Internet and information services; micro loans (as carried out in Bangladesh by Grameen) for faxes and computers; low-cost training courses; computer recycling for small businesses; e-commerce tool kits; networks; and newsletters.

The spotlight on tele-centers in Africa could be better off when modified from individual projects to developing a national system that supports an array of private, public, and small-scale projects to convey ICT within the reach of the majority in the continent. This would include:

- regulatory structure,
- business support and training,
- public-information and content-creation networks,
- access to loans,
- and technical assistance.

There is a market for telephony and there is evidence that ICTs can be useful in development, but yet to be fully and sustainably developed. The consequence should now be on supporting diverse initiatives while learning from them and sharing the experience. Big top-down projects have only limited use.

As ITU secretary-general Pekka Tarjanne has said: "The truth is that most Africans will not gain access to telecommunications without African initiatives, taken by individuals. The individual who sublets his or her phone line or sets up a phone shop or tele-center does more to close the development gap than the great corporations and businesses of the world" (Coetzee, 2007). There is very modest experience of the impact of such centers in the context of rural and remote areas in developing countries and there are many issues that need to be considered before one embarks on such ambitious and costly programs at the national level. Some of these issues of interest include:

- Defined rules of engagement for government institutions (information and telecommunications, education, health, agriculture, environment, trade and commerce, transport, etc.) and international organizations with established coordination mechanisms at national and international levels.
- Defined rules of engagement for local authorities and the private sector.
- Identification of the most cost-effective technology options for the various applications in the particular geographical, social and cultural environment and considering existing infrastructure.
- Determination of appropriate tariff structure with differentiated tariffs for commercial users and users of public services, as well as charges for services (smart cards, etc.).
- Determination of who pays for public services and how.
- Determination of the most viable options for public-private sector partnership and joint ventures.
- Determination of how and for what purpose are people using the facilities and what support is required.
- Determination of how to help people participate actively in the production of information, knowledge and art relevant to them (e.g., community information, such as job vacancies, information about social events, opinions on political and other issues, skill profiles, tourist information, artwork production, video programs, marketing information about their products, etc.).

- Determination of what information and communication facilities do people and government really need.
- Determination of what it takes to adapt information and learning material developed in the major languages of the world in affluent societies to the needs of generally poorly educated, often illiterate populations in rural and remote areas in developing countries. Is it at all possible? How can they cooperate with others in similar conditions (e.g., networking of community tele-centers).
- Determination of how to "market" Tele-center services in rural and remote areas and what are the effects of introducing community tele-centers on the development of the telecommunication markets in rural and remote areas.
- Determination of cost-effectiveness of different applications (telemedicine, tele-training, government and community information and decision support systems, trade and market information systems, environment protection, etc.), return on investment, including impact on social, economic and cultural development.
- Determination of how sustainability could be achieved.

At the World Telecommunication Development Conference (WTDC-94) the Buenos Aires Action Plan (BAAP) Program 9 – Integrated Rural Development[196] – a program that aims at establishing, in partnership with the private sector, a number of pilot projects in different developing regions and different geographical and cultural context, members of the ITU have attempted to address some of these issues.

---

196   Over 40% of the world's population lives in rural and remote areas of developing countries and have difficult or no access to even basic telecommunications services. Development of telecommunications in rural and remote areas therefore forms an important mission of the ITU Development sector. Pilot projects are projects sponsored by BDT, in collaboration with partners to demonstrate the feasibility of applications aimed at meeting the need of rural communities. Retrieved from http://www.fao.org/sd/CDdirect/CDre0042.htm

The pilot projects were a test bed for innovative applications such as tele-training and tele-medicine in the context of developing countries and provide opportunities for developing and testing distance learning material designed for poorly educated and illiterate people. The conception of such learning material and integration of existing information to local languages and culture would, incidentally, generate a number of jobs in developing countries.

Communities of practice (CoPs) are made relevant to support wide ranging knowledge management for robust international development and humanitarian actions, providing effective networks for generation and sharing of knowledge on selected issues in international development and humanitarian work. The CoPs are necessary especially when they are designed to address topics where exchange among individual field staff is needed to fill gaps in existing policy and technical guidance, and/or facilitate application of existing policy and guidance. Possible areas such CoPs can be built on are: humanitarian negotiations with non state entities, humanitarian accountability partnerships, gender equality in humanitarian action and disaster risk reduction.

As part of a wider UNICEF effort to strengthen its Knowledge Management (KM), for instance, the Office of Emergency Programs has undertaken a number of initiatives specially focused on KM to strengthen humanitarian action. One of these was the establishment of three Communities of Practices on: Humanitarian Negotiations with Non State Entities Gender Equality in Humanitarian Action and Disaster Risk Reduction[197].

Communities of Practice[198] are understood to be a network of individuals who share and accumulate their collective learning around a

---

197   The CCCs e-resource provides users with a consolidation of existing guidance on how to implement the revised CCs. For each area of the CCC, it offers easy accessibility to key existing policies, guidance and tools from UNICEF and partners. Retrieved from http://www.unicefinemergencies.com/downloads/eresource/Landing_Page.html

198   From the time our ancestors lived in caves to that day in the late '80s when Chrysler sanctioned unofficial "tech clubs" to promote the flow of information between teams working on different vehicle platforms, bands of like-minded individuals had been gathering in a wide variety of settings

common topic of interest; they deepen their knowledge and expertise by interacting on an ongoing basis (Wenger 2002). For the three CoPs in humanitarian action additional emphasis has been given to the immediacy of practical support. They contribute to strengthening organizational performance.

There are Communities of Practice functionalities maintained at the 'Emergencies Portal' (E-Portal) of UNICEF launched in 2009 which offers a one-stop shop or consolidated entry-way to all Intranet resources spanning EW and preparedness, humanitarian action and post-crisis recovery. There are a range of proposed updates and revisions proposed to the UNICEF E-portal to ensure continued coherence in the resources made available to staff. The E-portal and the three Communities of Practice pilots are intended to support wider knowledge management for stronger humanitarian action. Specifically, the objective of the Communities of Practice is to link knowledge to practice and support instant problem solving, collaboration and application of new learning.

The key tasks and processes in the evolution of all communities of practice involve the following:

---

to recount their experiences and share their expertise. Few paid much attention until a number of possible benefits to business were identified, but many are watching more closely now that definitive links have been established. In *Cultivating Communities of Practice*, consultants Etienne C. Wenger, Richard McDermott, and William Snyder take the concept to another level by describing how these groups might be purposely developed as a key driver of organizational performance in the knowledge age. Building on a 1998 book by Wenger that framed the theory for an academic audience, *Cultivating Communities of Practice* targets practitioners with pragmatic advice based on the accumulating track records of firms such as the World Bank, Shell Oil, and McKinsey & Company. Starting with a detailed explanation of what these groups really are and why they can prove so useful in managing knowledge within an organization, the authors discuss development from initial design through subsequent evolution. They also address the potential "dark side"--arrogance, cliquishness, rigidity, and fragmentation among participants, for example--as well as measurement issues and the challenges inherent in initiating these groups company-wide. (Howard Rothman). Retrieved from http://www.amazon.com/Cultivating-Communities-Practice-Etienne-Wenger/dp/1578513308

- Maintain support mechanisms capable of facilitating and consolidating appropriate responses to incoming queries in liaison with Policy/Technical Experts and most relevant Community Members and posting responses to the electronic platform to benefit the entire community.

- Maintain support mechanisms relaying longer term technical support requests to Policy/Technical Experts, tracking and documenting for the wider CoP the response.

- Maintain the collective community support mechanism, facilitating discussions as requested by CoP members, Policy and Technical Experts. This also entails supporting Policy Experts in developing and implementing discussion plans—helping to identify key product-oriented discussions that will further knowledge development within the CoPs, facilitating these and working with the Policy/Technical Experts to finalize products.

- Maintain CoP online tools (One-Stop-Shop and the Filtered Library) incorporating new material and maintaining existing material up to date in close consultation with Policy and Technical Experts and CoP members.

- Explore the possibility of developing a newsletter (bi-weekly or monthly newsletter) that goes out to all CoP members for each of the COPs. Design the concept of the news letter, the content and the mode for dissemination. The development of the news letter should be conducted in close collaboration with the members.

- Contribute to the review of the CoP experience and development of a longer-term strategy for all CoPs, consulting with CoP members on the usefulness of the CoPs and inviting suggestions for improvements.

- Maintain and develop wider electronic knowledge platforms for humanitarian/recovery (Intranet, shared drive and document repository, and possibly Internet) providing support on developing design changes to meet user needs and working with technical staff to implement them.

The multipurpose community tele-center projects provide also an ideal framework for piloting cross-sectoral, interdisciplinary and inter-agency cooperation. ITU is a membership organization always seeking new ideas from any persons interested in joining as partners in viable projects. Private sector members of the ITU/BDT and the Spacecom project sponsored by representatives of the satellite communication industry have indicated their keen interest in participating in these projects. The ITU 'Initiative 2000' has since allocated resources for such pilot projects over and above those provided under the BAAP Program No. 9. Other initiatives such as InfoDev, the AIF and the System-wide Special initiative for Africa are aiming at similar objectives. Clearly, therefore, there is an opportunity to implement multipurpose community tele-center projects if other agencies, including concerned UN organizations, bilateral development agencies and NGOs, are willing to contribute with support in their specific field of activity and to coordinate their activities aimed at rural community development with the implementation of such projects.

Chapter 11: Summary

OCL offers useful mechanisms for NGOs in developing countries to fulfill accountability obligations to a range of stakeholders, including beneficiaries of services, in a transparent, bottom-up manner. Many, however, argue that drilling wells for clean water, building roads, provision of primary health care and schools for teaching people to read and write are much more important for improving poor people's health and living conditions in general than providing them with computers and access to data networks. But so are the potential benefits of the "information society". Access to telephones and faxes reduces the need for people to travel and their feeling of being isolated and improves the efficiency of transportation of goods and services. Thus, telecommunications tools reduce transportation costs, improve availability of essential goods and services, and contribute to improving living conditions and to reducing pollution. Telecommunication tools may also contribute to saving lives in case of man-made or natural disasters and reduce the harmful consequences of such disasters.

Nobody questions the vital importance of schools and primary health care centers in rural and isolated communities. However, it is difficult to attract qualified teachers and doctors to work in such areas when there are no means of keeping in touch with colleagues and friends and with developments in their fields (except, possibly, by means of postal services which can take a long time to deliver a message or a book). The quality of public services, including health, education and security could be immensely improved by means of modern information and telecommunication technologies. Access to the rapidly increasing, electronically stored information and knowledge resources in the field of health and education, including courses in basic hygiene, literacy, water management and environment protection as well as in occupational fields of relevance to rural communities such as agriculture, animal husbandry, handicrafts, business administration, etc., and the possibility to call the specialist doctor when needed, are as important for the well being of the people as drilling wells and providing primary health centers. Access to such facilities would also contribute to retaining qualified professionals and attract more of them to work in rural and remote areas, i.e. reduce the migration to urban centers or even reverse this trend.

Access to information and communication technologies is vital for economic development and for any enterprise to compete in today's global economy, and generation of economic wealth and a more equal distribution of this wealth, within countries and globally, is equally critical for the poor to improve their living conditions; as well critical for social and cultural development. The advantages of access to information and "knowledge networks" and the possibility and right to communicate freely globally, by far outweighs any potential dangers of information technology. The right to communicate is a fundamental condition for the development of democracy and for global peaceful coexistence.

Multipurpose community tele-centers offer the means to make information services widely accessible to populations in remote and isolated rural areas, as well as in urban quarters and slums. The effect on social, economic and cultural development of these information networks is an integral part of a concerted effort of community development effort that should involve all stakeholders, including local authorities and user groups, international and national organizations, governmental as well as non-governmental organizations and the private sector concerned with community development and the development of new markets. When computer networks are available, people quickly become comfortable with using them, the collaboration seems to happen often and quickly in many disciplines and work groups. Telecommunication capabilities are today first-generation low-end wide area networking, with communication made with modems over international telephone connections or remote-connection Public Packet-Switched Data Network (PPSDN) links. And essential communications patterns have become decentralized with logins to regional central computers. As computer costs dropped and modem technologies improved to permit data communications over low-quality lines at higher speeds and plausible costs, opportunities arose for computer-computer connections, with people receiving and composing mail on their local systems, rather than trying to type while connected to remote locations.

Organizations can now establish single-purpose polled or dial-ut arrangements, typically using FidoNet[199] or Unix-to-Unix Copy (UUCP) technology, that link the components of that organization, or the collaborators in a particular project, with each other. In any given situation, this may be reasonable and the arrangements can be established with a minimum of fuss.

National governments all over the world are adopting e-Government initiatives. Services are now being offered via the Internet and allow citizens, businesses, and government employees to use self-service to search for jobs, apply for security clearances, file taxes electronically, apply for government grants, and take advantage of recreational opportunities. The United States Federal Government's vision for electronic government, for instance, is to make government more citizen-centered, results-oriented, and market-based. This program, championed by the Executive Office of the President[200], is now extending beyond the first wave of e-Government initiatives and is currently consolidating the back-office transactions in human resources and financial management services into centers of excellence.

The concept of shared services using OCL technologies has become broadly accepted in many governments and across many business functions. One source performed 143 interviews with personnel from eleven agencies in thirteen countries (United States, United Kingdom, Australia, South Africa, France, Canada, Sweden, Singapore, Italy, Germany, Ireland, Netherlands, and Spain). This source reports "66 percent of the governments surveyed have already implemented shared services or are in the process of implementing it. Another 28 percent anticipate

---

199   FidoNet consists of approximately 10,000 systems world-wide which comprise a network which exchanges mail and files via Modems using a proprietary protocol. They are connected for the purposes of exchanging E-Mail to the Internet thru a series of gateway systems which interact with the Internet via UUCP with cooperating UNIX-based smart-hosts which act as their MX-receivers. Retrieved from http://www.fidonet.org/

200   United States Office of Personnel Management. (2010). Human resources line of business. A collection of practices for human resources shared services and service delivery. http://www.opm.gov/egov/documents/practices/Collection_of_Practices.pdf

implementing shared services in the next one to three years. Only six percent have no plans to implement shared services. A majority of governments consider shared services using OCL technologies a vital tool for meeting their challenges and are investing considerable resources on their shared services operations. In fact, 85 percent of the governments surveyed believe shared services are or will be important to supporting their organization's strategic goals. Governments are effectively setting the tone, by providing policy statements in support of programs to bridge the digital divide, and acknowledging working models. They can assist developing world governments support Internet-friendly policies through the provision of expertise, training and aid to policy makers who are responsible for such legislation. The Digital Peace Corps idea proposed by various governments to provide technologists with an interest in doing socially responsible technology work abroad is a good idea as long as it is managed appropriately and real deliverables can be assessed.

References

Afele, J.S.C. (2002). Digital Bridges: Developing Countries in the Knowledge Economy. IGI Global.

Allison, J.E. (ed). 2002. Technology, Development, and Democracy: International Conflict and Cooperation in the Information Age. Albany, NY: SUNY.

Anderson, T & Hanuka, H. (1997). Online fora: new platforms for professional development and group collaboration. Journal of Computer Mediated Communication, 3 (3).

Awio, G., Lawrence, S., & Northcott, D. (2007). Community-led initiatives: reforms for better accountability? Journal of Accounting & Organizational Change, 3(3), 209–226.

Bade, K.J. & Anderson, L. (1994). Immigration and Social Peace in United Germany. Daedalus Kollock: London: Routledge.

Beaudin, P. (1999). Keeping Online Asynchronous Discussions on Topic. Journal of Asynchronous Learning Network, (9)1, 23–39.

Bélanger, M. (2005). Online Collaborative Learning. Retrieved July 21 2009 from http://training.itcilo.it/actrav/library/ english/ publications/online_cl.doc

Benbunan-Fich, R. & Hiltz, S.R. (1999). Impacts of asynchronous learning networks on individual and group problem-solving: A field experiment. In Group Decision and Negotiation. Dordrecht: Kluwer Academic Publishers.

Bereiter, C., & Scardamalia, M. (2003). „Learning to Work Creatively with Knowledge" In: E. De Corte, L. Verschaffel, N. Entwistle, & J. van Merriënboer (eds.), Unravelling Basic Components and Dimensions of Powerful Learning Environments. EARLI Advances in Learning and Instruction Series.

Bhargava, R. & Acharya, A. (2008). Political theory: an introduction. Pearson Education India

Bhattacharaya, M. (1999). A study of asynchronous and synchronous discussion on cognitive maps in a distributed learning environment. WebNet 99 World Conference on the World Wide

Web and Internet Proceedings, Honolulu, HI. (ERIC Document Reproduction No. ED448698).

Bovens, M. (2005). Public accountability. A framework for the analysis and assessment of accountability arrangements in the public domain. Paper presented at the Connex conference, Belfast 22 Sept.

Brown, L. K., & Troutt, E. (2007). Reporting Does Not Equal Accountability! The Importance of Funding Characteristics and Process on Accountability. International Journal of Public Administration, 30(2), 209–225.

Buck, L., Wollenberg, E., & Edmunds, D. (2001). Social learning in the collaborative management of community forests: Lessons from the field. In E. Wollenberg et al. (Eds.). Social Learning in Community Forestry, 1(20).

Cairncross, F. (1997). The death of distance: how the communication revolution will change our lives. Boston: Harvard Business School Press.

Chonia, G. H. (2002). The genesis of the promised LAN. University of Zurich, Switzerland. Retrieved from http://users.dec.uwi.edu/smarshall/itira/proceedings_online/2002/papers/developing_countries/chonia.pdf. Collis, B., & Margaryan, A. (2004). Applying activity theory to computer-supported collaborative learning and work-based activities in corporate settings. Educational Technology Research and Development, 52(4), 38–52.

Coetzee, L. (2007). World Wide Webs: Crossing the Digital Divide through Promotion of Public Access. University of Stellenbosch, South Africa. Retrieved from http://www.iisi.de/fileadmin/IISI/upload/C_T/2007/Coetzee.pdf

Department of Economic and Social Affairs. (2006). Open Access for Africa: Challenges, Recommendations and Examples. Department of Economic and Social Affairs.

D'Costa, A. & Sridharan, E. (2004). India in the global software industry. Palgrave Macmillan

Dillenbourg, P., & Schneider, D. (1995). Collaborative learning and the internet. Retrieved from: http://tecfa.unige.ch/tecfa/research/CMC/colla/iccai95_1.html.

Docquier, F. & Rapoport, H. (2007). Skilled migration: the perspective of developing countries, CReAM Discussion Paper Series. Centre for Research and Analysis of Migration (CReAM), Department of Economics, University College London.

Dose of Digital. (2010). The 7 Cs of Social Media Usage. Retrieved from http://www.doseofdigital.com/2010/02/ the-seven-uses-social-media-business/

Dringus, L. & Terrell, S. (1998). Awareness as a metaphor in online learning environments. Paper presented at the International Conference on Technology and Education (ICTE), Santa Fe, New Mexico.

Ebrahim, A. (2003). Accountability In Practice: Mechanisms for NGOs. World Development, 31(5), 813.

Ebrahim, A. (2005). Accountability Myopia: Losing Sight of Organizational Learning. Nonprofit and Voluntary Sector Quarterly, 34(1), 56–87.

Flack, T., & Ryan, C. (2005). Financial Reporting by Australian Nonprofit Organisations: Dilemmas Posed by Government Funders. Australian Journal of Public Administration, 64(3), 69–77.

Francescato, D., Mebane, M., Porcelli, R., Attanasio, C., & Pulino, M. (2007). Developing professional skills and social capital through computer supported collaborative learning in university contexts. International Journal of Human-Computer Studies, 65(2), 140–152.

Fowler, A. (1997). Striking a balance: A guide to enhancing the effectiveness of NGOs in international development. Earthscan.

Gakuru, M. & Stepman, F. (2009). Innovative Farmer Advisory Services using ICT. Forum for Agricultural Research in Africa. Retrieved from http://www.w3.org/2008/10/ MW4D_WS/

papers/fara.pdf.

Gibelman, M., & Gelman, S. R. (2001). Very Public Scandals: Non-governmental Organizations in Trouble. Voluntas: International Journal of Voluntary and Nonprofit Organizations, 12(1), 49–66.

Gibelman, M., & Gelman, S. R. (2004). A Loss of Credibility: Patterns of Wrongdoing Among Nongovernmental Organizations. Voluntas: International Journal of Voluntary and Nonprofit Organizations, 15(4), 355–381.

Gilbert, H. (1994). The Complete Cyberspace Reference and Directory: An Addressing and Utilization Guide to the Internet, Electronic Mail Systems, and Bulletin Board Systems. Wiley.

Global Governance Watch (2009). NGO Watch. Retrieved 27 September 2009, from http://www.globalgovernancewatch.org/ngo_watch/

Goddard, A., & Assad, M. J. (2006). Accounting and navigating legitimacy in Tanzanian NGOs. Accounting, Auditing & Accountability Journal, 19(3), 377–404.

Governance World Watch. (2007). Compiled and edited by the knowledge management branch of DPADM/UNDESA. Retrieved from http://www.unpan.org/directory/worldNews/include/ displayIssueDetail.asp?issueID=36 2233.

Gray, R., Bebbington, J., & Collison, D. (2006). NGOs, civil society and accountability: making the people accountable to capital. Accounting, Auditing & Accountability Journal, 19(3), 319–348.

Grimes, A., Bednar, M., Bolter, J. D., & Grinter, R. E. (2008). EatWell: sharing nutrition-related memories in a low-income community. Paper presented at the Proceedings of the ACM 2008 conference on Computer supported cooperative work.

Gurstein, M. (2000). Community informatics enabling communities with information and communications technologies . Hershey. PA: Idea Group Publishers.

Hamelink, C. J . (1997). New Information and Communication on Technologies, Social Development and Cultural Change.

Geneva: United Nations Research Institute for Social Development.

Harasim, L., et. al. (1995). Learning networks: a field guide to teaching and learning online. Cambridge, MA: MIT Press.

IFAD. (2010). Pastoral and Common Resources in Africa: Some IFAD Experiences and Lessons. Retrieved from http://www.ifad.org/lrkm/theme/range/pastoral.htm

International Non-Governmental Organisations (2005). Accountability Charter. Retrieved 15 June 2007, from http://www.realizingrights.org/pdf/INGO_Accountability_Charter.pdf

ITU (2010). Partnership on measuring ICT for development: Core ICT indicators 2010. Retrieved from http://www.itu.int/dms_pub/itu-d/opb/ind/D-IND-ICT_CORE-2010-PDF-E.pdf

Jones, S. (2003). An essential reference to communication and technology: Encyclopedia of New Media. Sage Publications

Kahn, R.L. (2000). The effect of technological innovation on organizational structure: two case studies of the effects of the introduction: a new technology on informal organizational structures. Journal of Business and Technical Communication, (14)328.

Keen, M., Brown , V., & Dyball, R. (Eds.) (2005). Social learning in environmental management: Towards a sustainable future. London: Earthscan.

Kelly, D. (2005). Power and participation: Participatory resource management in south-west Queensland. PhD thesis, Australian National University, Canberra.

Kirschner, P. A. (2004). Design, development, and implementation of electronic learning environments for collaborative learning. Educational Technology Research and Development, 52(3), 39–46.

Korten, D. (1990). Getting to the 21st century: Voluntary action and the global agenda. West Hartford, CT: Kumarian Press.

Kraut, R. et al. (1998). Social impact of the internet: what does it mean? Communications of the ACM, (41)12, 21–22.

Kumar, N. & Chadha, A. (2002). Exploiting the potential of information and communication technologies for development in South Asia. Sage Publications.

Kumar, R. & Sharma, V. (2005). Auditing principles and practice. Prentice-Hall of India Private Limited New Delhi.

Lai, L., & Turban, E. (2008). Groups Formation and Operations in the Web 2.0 Environment and Social Networks. Group Decision and Negotiation, 17(5), 387–402.

Leeuwis, C. (2000). Re-conceptualizing participation for sustainable rural development: Towards a negotiation approach. Development and Change, 31(5), 931–960.

Madon, S. (2000). International NGOs: networking, information flows and learning. Elsevier Science B.V. Retrieved from http://unpan1.un.org/intradoc/groups/public/documents/NISPAcee/UNPAN015542.pdf.

Madon, S. (2000). The Internet and socio-economic development: Exploring the interaction. Information Technology & People, 13(2), 85–101.

Mahmood, K. (2005). Multipurpose community telecenters for rural development in Pakistan. The Electronic Library, 23(2), 204–220.

McGregor-Lowndes, M., & Ryan, C. (2009). Reducing the Compliance Burden of Non-profit Organisations: Cutting Red Tape. Australian Journal of Public Administration, 68(1), 21–38.

Mele, C. (1999). Cyberspace and disadvantaged communities: The Internet as a tool for collective action. In Communities in Cyberspace. London: Routledge.

Meyer, C. A. (1997). The political economy of NGOs and information sharing. World Development, (25), 1127–1140.

Microsoft. (2008). Microsoft announces partnerships in Latin America to transform education and expand access to technology. Retrieved http://www.microsoft.com/presspass/press/2008/apr08/04 03POETAPR.mspx?rss_fdn=Press%20Releases.

Miller, F.P., Vandome, A., & McBrewster, J. (2009). Tiananmen Square protests of 1989: Tiananmen Square protests of 1989, Revolutions of 1989, Tiananmen Square, May Fourth Movement,

Tiananmen Incident, Government of the People's Republic of China. Alphascript Publishing.

Mills, Kurt. (2002). Cybernations: identity, self-determination, democracy, and the 'Internet Effect' in the emerging information order. Global Society, (16), 69–87.

Motsoaledi, P. (1997). The penetration of new technologies into developing countries: Cultural hegemony or mutual exchange? Prospects, 27(3), 385–392.

Munyua, H. (2007). ICTs and small-scale agriculture in Africa: a scoping study. IDRC. Retrieved from http://www.idrc.ca/uploads/user-S/12212542261Final_Report_HMunya.pdf.

Negroponte, N. (2009). One laptop per child: Mission Statement Retrieved November 21, 2009, from http://laptop.org/en/vision/mission/index.shtml

Norris, P. (2001). Digital Divide: Civic Engagement, Information Poverty, and the Internet Worldwide (Kindle Edition). Cambridge University Press.

One World Trust (2009). Making global governance more accountable Retrieved 27 September 2009, from http://www.oneworldtrust.org/

Poster, M. (1997). Cyberdemocracy: Internet and the public sphere. In Internet Culture. London: Routledge.

Preece, J. (2000). Online communities. Chichester: John Wiley.

Preston, W. & Herman, E.S. (1989). Hope and folly: the United States and UNESCO, 1945–1985. University of Minnesota Press.

Quibria, M.G. (2002). New Information and Communication Technologies and Poverty: Some evidence from developing Asia. Journal of the Asia Pacific Economy, 7(3).

Redden, G. (2001). Networking Dissent: The Internet and the Anti-Globalization Movement. Available at http://www.arts.uwa.edu.au/MotsPluriels/MP1801gr .html.

Roberts, T.M. (2004). Online collaborative learning: theory and practice. Idea Group, Inc.

Salamon. L.M., et al. (2001). Global civil society: dimensions of the nonprofit sector. Center for Civil Society Stuzles Publications, Johns Hopkins University.

Salamon, L. (1994). Partners in public service: Government—nonprofit relations in the modern welfare state. Baltimore, MD. Johns Hopkins.

Schuler, D. (1996). New community networks: wired for change. New York: Addison-Wesley Publishing Company.

Sen, A. & Drèze, J. (1999). The Amartya Sen and Jean Drèze Omnibus: (comprising) poverty and famines; hunger and public action; India: economic development and social opportunity. Oxford University Press: USA

Sherry, L. & Wilson, B. (1997). Transformative communication as a stimulus to Web innovations. Web-Based Instruction. Educational Technology Publications, Englewood Cliffs.

SIDA. (2009). ICTs for democracy: Information and communication technologies for the enhancement of democracy—with a focus on empowerment.
Retrieved from http://www.apc.org/en/system/files/ SIDA_ICTs+for+Democracy.pdf.

Siegel, M. A. and Kirkley, S. (1997). Moving toward the digital learning environment: the future of web-based instruction. Web-Based Instruction. Educational Technology Publications, Englewood Cliffs, NJ.

Slim, H. (2002, January 10–12, 2002). By What Authority?: The Legitimacy and Accountability of Non-governmental Organisations. Paper presented at the The International Council on Human Rights Policy International Meeting on Global Trends and Human Rights, Geneva.

Smillie, I., & Hailey, J. (2001). Managing for change: Leadership, strategy and management in Asian NGOs. London: Earthscan.

Smillie, I. (1999). Narrowing the digital divide notes on a global Netcorps: Information and communication technologies and development. UNITeS Resource Center.

Smillie, I. (1995). The alms bazaar: Altruism under fire— Nonprofit organizations and international development. London: Intermediate Technology.

Smith, J. (2009). Facebook Surpasses 175 Million Users, Continuing to Grow by 600k Users/Day, Retrieved 25 October 2009 from http://www.insidefacebook.com/ 2009/02/14/facebook-surpasses-175-million-users-continuing-to-grow-by-600k-usersday/

Smith, S. & Lipsky, M. (1993). Non-profits for hire: the welfare state in the age of contracting. Cambridge, MA: Harvard University Press.

South China Morning Post. (1995). The net will follow, not lead, China's reforms. Retrieved from http://cyber.law.harvard .edu/ archived_content/people/edelman/pubs/scmp 012603.pdf.

Spence, R. (2003). Background Paper: Discussion, Research, Collaboration – Information and Communications Technologies (ICTs) for Poverty Reduction: When, Where and How? IDRC.

Srebeny, S. & Khiabany, G. (2010). Blogistan: The Internet and Politics in Iran. Tauris

Srikantaiah, T. K. & Koenig, E.D. (2008). Knowledge Management in Practice: Connections and Context. Information Today, Inc.

Stone, B. (2009, 10 December). Facebook's Privacy Changes Draw More Scrutiny. New York Times. from http://bits.blogs. nytimes.com/2009/12/10/facebooks-privacy-changes-draw-more-scrutiny/.

SUR: International Journal of Human Rights. (2009). Perpetrating Good: Unintended Consequences of International Human Rights Advocacy. Retrieved from http://www.surjournal.org/ eng/conteudos/getArtigo9.php?artigo=9,artigo_bukovska. htm

Tomei, L.A. (2009). Information communication technologies for enhanced education and learning: advanced applications and development. IGI Global.

Tu, C.H. (2004). Online collaborative learning communities: twenty-one designs to building an online learning collaborative learning community. CT: Libraries Unlimited.

Turoff, M. (1978). Development and field testing of an Electronic Information Exchange System: final report on the EIES development project. New Jersey Institute of Technology, Newark, N.J.

Turoff, M. & Hiltz, R. (1977). How to use EIES, Electronic Information Exchange System. Computerized Conferencing and Communications Center, New Jersey Institute of Technology.

TweetDeck (2009). from http://tweetdeck.com/

Unerman, J., & O'Dwyer, B. (2006). On James Bond and the importance of NGO accountability. Accounting, Auditing & Accountability Journal, 19(3), 305–318.

Vakil, A. (1997). Confronting the classification problem: Towards a taxonomy of NGOs. World Development 25(12): 2057–2071.

Verdejo, M. F. (1996). Interaction and collaboration in distance learning through computer mediated technologies. Advanced educational technology: Research issues and future technologies. Berlin: Springer-Verlag.

Walsh, J.P. & Shaul, G. (1997). Social networks in the age of the Internet. Conceptual and methodological Issues. Paper presented at the American Sociological Association Annual Meeting, Toronto.

Warkentin, C. (2001). Reshaping world politics: NGOs, the Internet, and global civil society. Lanham, MD: Rowman & Littlefield Publishers.

Washington Times. (2009). Editorial: Iran's Twitter Revolution – witnessing a new chapter in the quest for freedom. Retrieved from http://www.washingtontimes.com/ news/2009/jun/16/ irans-twitter-revolution/

Wenger, E.; McDermott, R.; & Snyder, W.M. (2002). Cultivating Communities of Practice. Harvard Business Press

White, C.S. (1997). Citizen participation and the Internet: prospects for civic deliberation in the Information Age. Social Studies, (88),1

Wilson, E.J. (1999). Meeting the challenges of Internet inequality.

Center for International Development and Conflict management, University of Maryland.World Bank. (2012). WDI 2012. The World Bank Group. Retrieved from http://www.data.worldbank.org/data-catalog/world-development-indicators/wdi-2012

World Bank. (2011). Directions in Development—Private Sector Development: Fostering technology absorption in Southern African enterprises.

World Bank. (1998). World Development Report: Knowledge for development. Retrieved from http://www wds.worldbank.org/external/default/WDSContentServer/IW3P/IB/1998/11/17/0001788 0_98111703550058/Rendered/PDF/multi_page.pdf

Yao-Jen, C., Yu-Chia, C., Tsen-Yun, W., & Yao-Sheng, C. (2008). Assessing Online Behaviors through Discussion Forums in NGO's Daily Working Life. Paper presented at the Proceedings of the 2008 Third International Conference on Convergence and Hybrid Information Technology, Volume 01.

Index